D1438954

VIETNAM
THE SECRET WAR

VIETNAM
THE SECRET WAR
Kevin M Generous

Bison Books

First published in 1985 by
Bison Books Ltd
176 Old Brompton Road
London SW5
England

ISBN 0 86124 243 2

Printed in Hong Kong

Reprinted 1988

Page 1: *Operation Castor,
prelude to the battle of
Dienbienphu -- 24
November 1953.*
Pages 2-3: *Airmobile US
Cavalry in action near
Bong Son: Operation
White Wing, 1966.*
This page: *French soldiers
survey the ravaged
countryside around
Dienbienphu shortly before
their surrender.*

Contents

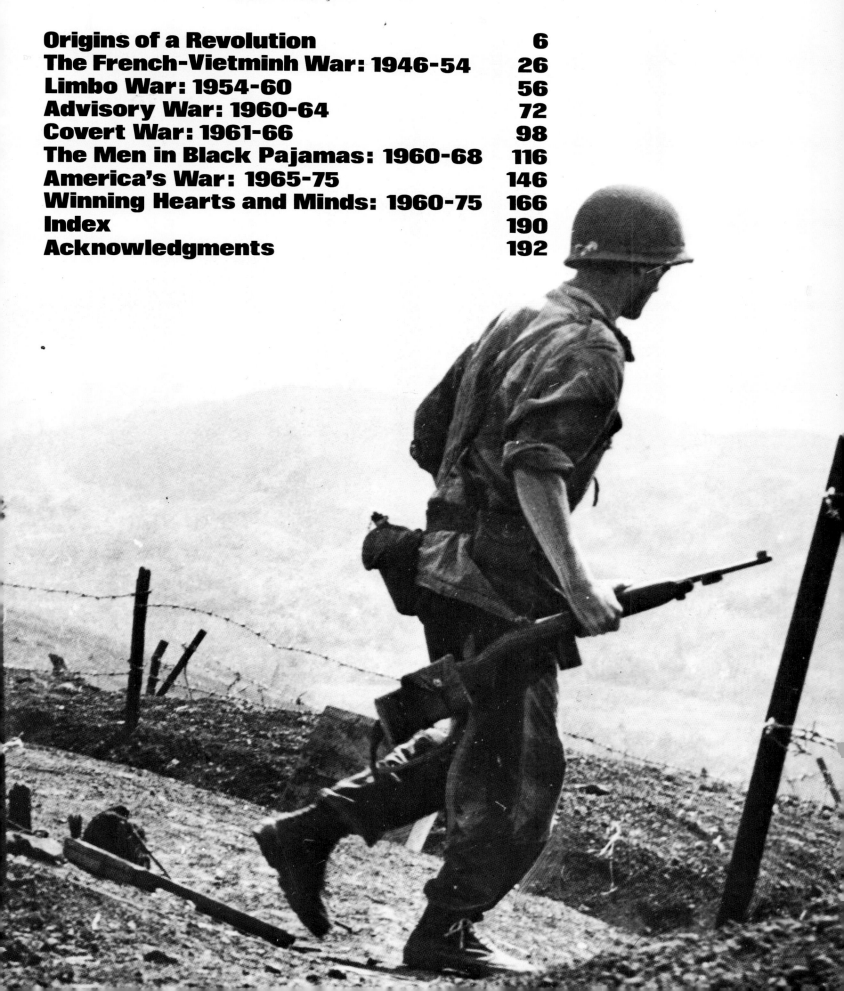

Origins of a Revolution

In Vienna – on the front lines of the Cold War during the late 1950s – the CIA station chief read an intriguing, highly classified cable. Its intended destination was Vientiane, Laos, but it had been misrouted to his station through an all-too-typical communications error.

The Central Intelligence Agency's Vienna station was at the hub of a complex cloak-and-dagger war between Soviet and American intelligence services. From his setting in the refined atmosphere of central Europe, the CIA chief directed a world of espionage, LeCarre-style: microfilm drops, double agents, and intellectual cat-and-mouse games with talented, dangerous Soviet counterparts.

Secret War in Asia

The Vientiane cable piqued the interest of the veteran intelligence officer, revealing to him a hitherto unknown side of covert war. In stark contrast to the gentlemanly Old-World environment of Vienna, a not-so-Cold War was raging on the other side of the world – a war of secret weapon drops by parachute to remote, clandestine CIA guerrilla armies, surreptitious cross-border operations, omnipresent communist underground cells and distant jungle skirmishes by paramilitary groups of dubious loyalties.

The station chief, intrigued by this 'other war,' would soon be assigned to steamy Saigon, involved in a largely unknown war fought between two great Western military powers and Asian communist revolutionaries.

By all twentieth-century Western military standards, the two Vietnam wars were 'unconventional.' Western military leaders faced agrarian-based guerrillas from an undeveloped colonial society, primitive in weapons and tactics, with no real military traditions, modern transport, or air force. While Western commanders anticipated an easy campaign, Ho Chi Minh's insurgents steadfastly refused to fight a European-style war of maneuver, relying instead on traditional guerrilla tactics – stealth, surprise, ambush and deception – perfectly adapted to local geography, climates and customs.

During 1500 years of battle against occupation by powerful Chinese neighbors, the Vietnamese had developed a tradition of protracted guerrilla fighting. Vietnamese General Tran Hung Dao, who defeated the dreaded Mongols in 1278, defined a guerrilla strategy which, 700 years later, would inspire Ho Chi Minh's insurgents: 'The enemy must fight his battles far from his home base...we must further weaken him by drawing him into protracted campaigns. Once his initial dash is broken, it will be easier to destroy him.'

To the Vietnamese tradition of insurgent warfare, Ho Chi Minh – the brilliant communist and nationalist – added a distinctive clandestine flavor. Ho blended fierce Vietnamese nationalism with a Marxist-Leninist organization, dominated by Mao Tse-tung's doctrine of 'revolutionary warfare' (guerrilla 'fish' swimming in a 'sea' of rural peasants). The result was a mystic, quasi-religious doctrine of *dau tranh* or 'struggle' which molded the Vietminh – and later the Vietcong – insurgent into a disciplined instrument with a single purpose: the elimination of Western influence in Southeast Asia.

Dau tranh legitimized armed terrorism, kidnapping and assassination.

A Western commentator once called the post-World-War-II Vietnam wars a clash between two distinct military philosophies, one based on the mobility of the individual soldier, the other on the mobility of professional armies. But beneath the well-documented failures of conventional Western military strategy in Southeast Asia lies another story of how a few creative Western soldiers and intelligence operatives adapted to the rigors of combat in the inhospitable jungles, mountains and swamps of Indochina.

When conventional military methods proved inadequate, these innovative Cold Warriors – often bucking the conventional tide of their respective organizations – worked to adapt special techniques to defeat revolutionary warfare and the Vietnamese offshoot, 'people's warfare.' Unconventional missions like pacification (clearing a given region of insurgents), intelligence collection and special

Above: *A Montagnard is questioned by a member of the 173rd Airborne Brigade during a search-and-destroy mission at Pleiku.*
Right: *Chiang Kai-shek, leader of the Nationalist Chinese forces who had to retreat to Formosa (Taiwan) before Mao Tse-tung's Communist armies.*
Opposite: *Weapons and provisions are laboriously hand-carried to the Vietnamese popular front during the fight against French domination (1951).*

Previous pages: *The newly signed accord on the independence of Vietnam is celebrated in a Saigon parade (1954).*

operations called for the development of unconventional units and methods, and spawned a crazy-quilt spectrum of irregular units: covert political-psychological ('psywar') teams, private tribal armies and paramilitary groups, counterguerrilla commandos and elite special-forces units. The collective mission of these irregulars was to fight the communist guerrilla at the rice-roots level.

A counterguerrilla war waged at this level by Westerners, however, had its disadvantages. While Ho Chi Minh had a clear vision, a specially adapted organization and specific methods to achieve his goal, the Western unconventional warrior did not. By virtue of Western training and support, Southeast Asia's noncommunist armies reflected the conventional bent of its sponsors and thus forced the unconventional warrior either to duplicate the successful aspects of people's war or experiment with his own. Many irregular units and tactics sprang up in an *ad hoc* way, the result of constant tinkering in the field. What worked remained in operation; what did not was dropped for something that did.

Such improvisation, however, often led to controversial methodology – 'deniable' covert actions across international boundaries and assassination of secret communist cadres, for example – deemed by critics to be inconsistant with, and alien to, the principles of Western society, even though the other side routinely employed such methods. But to the practicioners, who best understood the brutal reality and violence of people's warfare, who fought and died beside resisting tribesmen, all was fair in the course of a bloody, no-holds-barred secret war.

The Foreign Legion and the *Deuxieme Bureau*

The colonies France established in Indochina after 1858 held great strategic value as France's 'Balcony on the Pacific,' initially to counter British interests in the Far East and later as a foothold into the vast Chinese commercial markets. Military conquests of Indochina had been almost painless: a few French gunboats had cruised up the Red River in 1883 with 5000 Foreign Legionnaires to defeat 20,000 Chinese at Son Tay fortress. The Legionnaires easily pushed the Chinese out of Vietnam and by 1884, France held sway in Tonkin (northern Vietnam) and eventually all of Indochina.

Pesky bands of Vietnamese guerrillas occasionally kept the French mercenaries occupied. The first of many roving rebel groups in the Tonkinese hills, led by a patriotic Confucianist, Phan Dinh Phung, was finally crushed by the Foreign Legion in the mid-1880s. Foreign Legionnaires, enticed by Vietnamese *choum* (native rice alcohol) and *congai* (beautiful and devoted Vietnamese wives and mistresses), became a firm fixture for the next 70 years, the most visible symbol of French military supremacy in the region. But it was the unseen French security service, the *Deuxieme Bureau of the Surete* (police), that oversaw the activities of Vietnamese nationalist groups. The *Surete*'s extensive informant network and vigilant police techniques enabled the effective combination of French police and Foreign Legion troops to crush any nationalist uprising before it became too widespread or organized.

Deuxieme Bureau spies did not keep nationalists from trying; when the *Surete* closed down one organization, another popped up somewhere else. The best-known nationalist was born Nguyen Tat Thanh in 1890, the son of a scholar-official with strong anti-colonialist feelings. The young man traveled extensively as a cook on a French merchant ship, visiting Africa, Asia and even the United States. He too developed anti-colonial views and became involved in Vietnamese political activities in Paris, work that included presenting a demand for colonial self-determination to the Great Powers at the Versailles Peace Conference. In 1920, with a growing reputation as a revolutionary, the young Vietnamese changed his name to Nguyen Ai Quoc (Nguyen the Patriot), his pseudonym for the next quarter-century. But he would become more famous under the name of Ho Chi Minh.

'Nguyen the Patriot' also became a Marxist-Leninist. Summoned to Moscow in 1923, Ho worked for the Comintern at the 'Stalin School for the Toilers of the East,' a special academy for third-world revolutionaries, and formed a quasi-Marxist patriotic organization, the Revolutionary Youth League, in 1925. Based in Canton, out of the

Above: Montagnard *tribesmen pass in review during a 1965 parade in Saigon, Republic of Vietnam.*

Above: *Vietnamese peasants camouflage barbed wire in their campaign of resistance to the French.*

Secretary of State John Foster Dulles, whose 'domino theory' was instrumental in shaping US foreign policy in Southeast Asia during the 1950s and 1960s.

Bureau's grasp, the League operated under the auspices of China's ruling Kuomintang Government under Chiang Kai-shek, who was eager to foment anti-French sentiment in Indochina. Within the League's leadership, however, Ho secretly recruited a core of dedicated Marxist-Leninists – the nucleus of a future Indochinese Communist Party (ICP), formed in 1930.

Ho taught his followers that previous Vietnamese rebel groups had accomplished little by merely assassinating a few local colonial officials, with no co-ordination or support from the Vietnamese people. Ho promised that under 'the good leadership by the party,' the Vietnamese people could achieve a successful revolution.

Leninist doctrine, Ho wrote, would provide the tightly knit, clandestine organization. Protracted guerrilla warfare, the traditional form of Vietnamese resistance, would serve as the military strategy for revolution. The most cohesive revolutionary element – Vietnamese nationalism – would mobilize the peasantry. External support in the form of a 'great rear base' – which could nourish a guerrilla insurgency with arms and military training – was the only ingredient Ho lacked to begin his struggle

Above: *Members of the Vietminh General Headquarters Planning Section at work soon after the organization's establishment in the early 1940s.*

Opposite: *Ho Chi Minh (born Nguyen Tat Thanh), the dedicated Vietnamese Communist, whose first* nomme de guerre *was Nguyen Ai Quoc – 'the Patriot.' He studied and taught at Moscow's 'School for the Toilers of the East' in preparation for his career as a revolutionary.*

against the hated French colonialists.

The Communist Party's first real test, the 1930 Nghe Tinh Rebellion, proved a costly disaster. In September 1930, a local peasant rebellion broke out in Annam (central Vietnam), where communists encouraged peasants to seize land, annulled taxes and distributed rice. Communist cadres tried to channel the spontaneous uprising into a revolutionary movement by organizing angry peasants into local village associations (called soviets) and militias, armed with knives, spears and clubs.

Foreign Legionnaires put down the rebellion with great brutality, but not before a series of pitched battles between French and peasant militias in which thousands died. *Deuxieme Bureau* agents quickly squashed the rebellion by rounding up some 90 percent of the ICP leadership. French officials notified Hong Kong police of the ICP involvement and additional party members, including Ho Chi Minh, were arrested and imprisoned.

The communists rebuilt their shattered cadres over the next decade – under the watchful eye of intelligence men. French agents penetrating the Vietnamese revolutionary community knew the exact number of Vietnamese studying in Moscow's 'Stalin School.' During 1932, for example, French police rounded up 32 of the 40 Vietnamese 'alumni' of the previous year. Many were arrested upon arrival in Indochina and joined their colleagues in French prisons.

When the Vietnamese Communists tried turning French prisons, teeming with other non-communist radicals, into classrooms for teaching Communist doctrine, the *Deuxieme* simply placed double agents in the inmate population, so that the ICP could trust only 1 in 1000 ex-prisoners upon release.

As in so many other colonial territories worldwide, communist groups in Indochina were stymied by a well-entrenched, well-organized secret police that kept good informant networks and crushed local uprisings. Ho's followers would find that only a world war could loosen the *Surete*'s hold over communist activities in Vietnam.

Before her defeat by Nazi Germany in 1940, France's military supremacy in Indochina went unchallenged. But her ignominious collapse in Europe encouraged Japan to expand its 'Greater East Asia Co-prosperity Sphere' into French Indochina. In June 1940, the Japanese General Staff demanded that the French Governor General cut the railhead between Tonkin and China, knowing that American matériel from the port of Haiphong supplied Chiang Kai-shek's Kuomintang armies. The Vichy Government conceded to new Japanese demands-in August for the right to station troops in Tonkin. To ensure total French co-operation, Japanese troops briefly attacked the French frontier post at Langson in September 1940. Under the subsequent *Pax Nippon*, the Japanese allowed a French colonial administration in Indochina, but under the watchful eye of Japanese military authorities and the *Kempeitai*, the Japanese secret police.

Ho Chi Minh spent most of the 1930s in Moscow. In spring 1940, Ho finally contacted two dedicated young Vietnamese Communists, Vo Nguyen Giap (the future North Vietnamese Army Commander) and Pham Van Dong (future North Vietnamese Prime Minister). From these two men Ho discovered that communist forces were ill-prepared for what Ho viewed as a perfect opportunity to take advantage of France's bleak political situation in Indochina.

In Ho's absence, poorly trained communist guerrillas at Bac San had recklessly attacked French border garrisons – after the Japanese had wrung political concessions from the French in September 1940. Japanese officers watched as the Bac Son guerrillas were decimated in repeated head-on attacks on French outposts. In Cochin China, another premature and unco-ordinated uprising against the French was brutally suppressed after the *Surete* captured a regional party official, who divulged the revolutionary plan.

In May 1941, Ho Chi Minh and other ICP leaders met in the small border village of Pac Bo to discuss a new political-military strategy for defeating the French. Ho realized that Japanese expansion into Indochina meant diminished French power. With a US-Japanese clash in the Pacific seemingly inevitable, Ho believed that a credible Vietnamese nationalist organization could fill a temporary power vacuum in Indochina. It was decided to build a broad patriotic-front organization, pulling all nationalist groups into a 'League for the Independence of Vietnam' (*Viet Nam Doc Lap Dong Minh*), better known as the Vietminh.

Ho placed great emphasis on disguising the Communist Party's dominant role in the Vietminh – to broaded the front's nationalist appeal and to attract support from traditionally conservative and xenophobic rural villagers. Gone was the disastrous emphasis on frontal attacks and ineffective peasant uprisings. The revolution's success was pinned on the concept of a protracted guerrilla war – in short, a people's war.

Vietminh guerrillas began carving out a revolutionary base area in a remote and relatively inaccessible region, much like the rugged Yenan caves where Mao Tse-tung's forces trained after their famous 'Long March' of the 1930s. Tonkin's mountainous Viet Bac region north of Hanoi, long a traditional sanctuary for Vietnamese rebels, became the revolutionary base where selected guerrilla units trained under a Vietminh political organization, preparing to organize a broad-based people's war.

The decimated Bac Son remnants officially became 'the Army of National Salvation' in 1941. The 'army' consisted mainly of ethnic tribesmen with little formal military training. By 1943 the Bac Son movement comprised a few platoons of guerrillas, armed with little more than 50 weapons. The 400-man 'army' saw little combat, operating in dispersed teams, organizing village 'self-defense' militias in Vietminh-controlled areas.

Ho organized an entirely new military force at Cao Bang, 50 miles north of Bac Son. Vo Nguyen Giap, a former Hanoi history teacher with a strong interest in guerrilla tactics, was chosen to lead this rag-tag 'People's Liberation Army.' By 1943 Giap had mustered only 300-400 insurgents armed with grenades and flintlock rifles. This force accomplished little more than to consolidate Vietminh control in the 'liberated' Viet Bac – mostly because the Vietminh still lacked the external support essential for the revolution's success.

Ho Chi Minh arranged for this support in an unorthodox manner. While traveling incognito to a Chinese Communist Party (CCP) meeting in South China in 1942, Ho was captured by the anti-Communist Kuomintang secret police. In typically bold fashion, Ho proposed to a powerful Kuomintang warlord, General Chang Fa-k'uei, a plan to finance two Vietminh guerrilla bases in the Viet Bac to harass Japanese troops near the Chinese border. Ho requested 1000 rifles, machine guns, 4000 grenades and a cash subsidy. The warlord released Ho in September 1943, without the arms, but with a $50,000 monthly subsidy from the anti-Communist Kuomintang.

With this support, Giap fielded his first regular unit in December 1944, the 1st Armed Propaganda Detachment, consisting of 31 men and 3 women armed with 2 revolvers, 17 rifles, 14 flintlocks and one light machine gun. The detachment, designed primarily as a transitional unit to perform political and military functions, proved its mettle in combat by overrunning two French outposts in early 1945, and in scattered skirmishes with the Japanese.

Opposite: *Early Vietminh supply columns utilized bicycles to good effect, as did the Japanese in Burma during World War II.*
Near right: *A North Vietnamese attack on the French strongpoint at Dong Khe.*

Above: *A member of the French command confers with a representative of the Vietnamese Government.*

The demonstration of Giap's troops in combat took on added importance as the war turned in the Allies' favor in 1944. Ho wanted Allied recognition of the Vietminh as a formidable military and political force that could prevent resurgent French control after Japan's defeat. The secret external support Ho received from the Kuomintang provided some political leverage, but Ho needed broader Allied support and realized that the United States held the key to Vietnam's postwar independence.

Ho sensed that a unique opportunity to realize his lifelong goal was close at hand. A December 1944 Vietminh document noted that 'Our future will be undertaken in very favorable conditions ... it would be unpardonable for us not to take advantage of it.'

March Coup by the Japanese

By late 1944, the Japanese General Staff, well aware of their fragile hold on Indochina, began to dissolve the wartime relationship with the Vichy regime. The *Kempeitai* and the *Bureau* clashed over sponsorship of pro-Japanese Vietnamese militia, a policy designed to accelerate the dismantling of French colonial power – to the benefit of Vietnamese nationalists.

Kempeitai officials began arming Vietnamese auxiliary groups in Tonkin and the southern Cao Dai sect in late 1943. While the French could not openly confront Japanese policy, the *Deuxieme Bureau* tried to thwart Japanese-inspired Vietnamese nationalism. However, Vichy collaboration with Japan had already demonstrated French weakness; further activities against Vietnamese nationalists only poisoned the atmosphere for later French-Vietnamese dialogue.

With an eye on the activities of Charles de Gaulle's Free French forces, French colonial officials began to drift away from their Vichy collaboration in the hope of retaining power as agents of victorious Allies. By January 1945, a newly formed French underground began stockpiling arms parachuted by British Special Operations Executive (SOE), which supported clandestine Allied commando operations in the Far East. The *Kempeitai* easily caught wind of French preparations for armed insurrection – undertaken with an almost total lack of discretion. On 9 March 1945, in a lightning *coup d'état*, Japanese troops moved against French military and colonial administrative centers.

In what Legionnaires remember as 'the Night of the Samurai,' Imperial Japanese soldiers engaged in a gory slaughter of French troops. Over 4000 French troops were interned. A few French garrisons put up a tenacious resistance, but were surprised and brutally overwhelmed. At the Foreign Legion's Lang Son garrison, French officers found themselves staring down the gunbarrels of their Japanese dinner hosts. Those who resisted were swiftly dispatched with samurai swords, while a Legionnaire general was beheaded for refusing to surrender his command. The Japanese also took over the French colonial administrative apparatus, throwing many officials into prison. Within 24 hours, an organized Free French resistance in Indochina evaporated.

A single French command escaped the *Kempeitai*'s dragnet. Led by native guides, some 2000 Legionnaires of the 5th Regiment at Tong, northwest of Hanoi, led by Generals M Alessandri and C Sabattier, escaped due west into the rugged jungle interior, past 40,000 hostile Nippon troops in the Red River Delta. Japanese troops dogged the Legion column with constant ambushes in the steamy jungle mist, both sides frequently resorting to close-quarter fighting with bayonets, knives and rifle butts.

The regiment finally stumbled into Dienbienphu, an isolated outpost on the Laos-Vietnamese border, in late March, whence Alessandri put out an appeal to the Allies for arms and air support. General Claire Chennault, commander of the 14th US Army Air Force in China, received Alessandri's message and prepared to send help, but Chennault soon received countermanding orders from Washington: 'No arms and ammunition would be provided to French troops under any circumstances.' The French were on their own.

One American lieutenant, Robert Ettinger, flew into Dienbienphu to size up the combined French-Vietnamese forces, now numbering 5500. Ettinger worked for the Office of Strategic Services (OSS), the American clandestine warfare service. His was the first OSS team active in Indochina, its mission to

Above: *Japanese prisoners charged as war criminals arrive in Saigon from the Foreign Legion's Lang Son garrison, after the massacre known as the Night of the Samurai (9 March 1945).*

Left: *North Vietnamese artillery units like this one became skillful and effective in the early phases of what was originally known as the Indochina War.*

survey General Sabattier's troops to determine whether they might be employed for commando operations against the Japanese.

Lieutenant Ettinger accompanied the French forces as they marched from Dienbienphu north to China, harassed by Japanese ambushes, hunger, disease and a hostile Vietnamese population. A few 14th Air Force planes managed to strafe Japanese columns along Sabattier's line of retreat. The depleted French corps reached China in May 1945, completing a grueling 57-day march from Hanoi. Many troops were hospitalized immediately; the others were disarmed by Chinese troops. Many French soldiers told OSS officers that they only wanted to return to fight the Japanese.

In the wake of the March coup, the Japanese set up a puppet government under Vietnamese Emperor Bao Dai and granted it a paper independence, making a French return more difficult. This action removed the last vestiges of French colonial power, including the omnipotent *Bureau*. The power vacuum Ho had predicted in 1940 had now arrived.

Ho Chi Minh seeks OSS support

Eradication of French military and police influence left Ho's Vietminh the best-organized underground in Indochina. By June 1945, the Vietminh held six entire provinces in Tonkin, and had created an extensive intelligence network there, far superior to the disorganized Free French *maquis*. Ho was convinced that the American OSS needed the Vietminh as much as the Vietminh needed American sponsorship.

The OSS, based on the clandestine British SOE and MI-6, had achieved great success in behind-the-lines activities in virtually every theater of war. The true forerunner of the postwar Central Intelligence Agency, the OSS was divided into Secret Intelligence (SI), and Special Operations (SO) branches, engaged in a wide variety of activities, including

intelligence collection and analysis, espionage, sabotage, commando strikes and guerrilla and psychological warfare. In occupied Europe, the SO teams, nicknamed 'Jedburghs,' set up underground resistance groups. The OSS-backed *maquisards* (underground resistance fighters, from *maquis*, meaning clump of trees) performed invaluable services, sowing great confusion prior to the Allied invasion of Europe.

After the March coup, Washington authorized the OSS Far East headquarters in Kunming, China, to establish an intelligence network in Indochina and to render military aid 'in the form of supplies and/or US controlled military personnel to any and all groups opposing the Japanese forces.' OSS-Kunming took a pragmatic, apolitical view in supporting paramilitary groups, treating all groups, according to their orders, in a like manner 'irrespective of any political affiliations.' The sole criterion

Below: *A Japanese convoy sets out for the countryside to subdue resistance to the 1945 occupation.*

used by the OSS was to aid those groups best prepared to contribute to an Allied victory over Japan. While aware of the political leanings of a Mao Tsetung or a Ho Chi Minh, OSS officers needed local intelligence and approached those who could provide it.

By late 1944, Ho Chi Minh's intelligence network was supplying Allied sources with valuable information leading to the rescue of downed 14th Air Force pilots. Ho personally initiated contact with the OSS SI Branch in China early in 1945, offering intelligence on the Japanese in return for OSS arms and support. In a token of appreciation for their assistance in recovery of American airmen, the SI Branch chief sent the Vietminh six revolvers and 20,000 rounds of ammunition, but refused to supply more arms because Ho did not accept the condition that OSS guns were not to be turned against the French. However, to maintain relations with the embryonic guerrilla movement, a few American OSS liaison officers parachuted into the Viet Bac – over vigorous French objections.

As the war in Europe ended, de Gaulle's Free French *maquisards* attempted to re-establish intelligence networks in Southeast Asia independent of Allied services. One of these secret services, known as Mission 5 under Jean Sainteny, controlled the remnants of General Sabattier's corps – by then almost entirely dependent upon American logistical support. After extensive negotiations in June 1945, it was agreed that 25 French officers and 100 Vietnamese were to receive OSS commando training for joint Franco-American operations in Tonkin. Jean Sainteny objected strongly to the integration of Sabattier's *maquis* under OSS operational control. French-OSS co-operation was shaky at best. French officials, according to an OSS SI branch chief, 'were

infinitely more concerned with keeping Americans out of Indochina than they were with defeating the Japanese.' The OSS-trained commando units never played an important military role, with only a few operations actually launched before VJ Day.

One of these operations was a highly successful commando raid – code-named COMORE – against the Japanese 22nd Division at Lang Son in June 1945. COMORE consisted of five OSS sabotage experts and 100 French and Vietnamese commandos led by OSS Captain Lucien Conein, a French-speaking ex-Foreign Legionnaire. Under cover of darkness, Conein's team emerged from the jungle, blew up Japanese fuel and ammo dumps and captured two prisoners and a cache of documents before melting back into the jungle. COMORE reaped an intelligence bonanza on Japanese military operations in Southeast Asia while suffering only a single casualty.

OSS-Kunming hoped for many more COMORE-type operations in Tonkin. But Conein reported after the Lang Son raid that the Vietminh 'held the entire area from Lang Son to the Chinese frontier.' Another OSS officer observed that the local population's hatred of the French 'makes it a more dangerous place for them than for us.' De Gaulle's agents, demonstrating every intention of returning to the prewar colonial domination of Indochina, viewed the OSS-Vietminh contacts with growing suspicion, knowing the anti-colonialist feelings held by many American officers.

The continued intrigues of the French secret services led indirectly to greater OSS-Vietminh co-operation. While preparing another joint French-OSS mission in South China, Chinese and Vietnamese agents warned the mission commander, OSS Major Allison K Thomas, that he would 'find

the whole population against him' if accompanied by French troops, and that he risked being fired on by the local population. Thomas postponed his mission and parachuted into the Viet Bac on 16 July 1945 to investigate the charges. Accompanying Thomas was a five-man OSS advance team and a French officer in disguise.

'Welcome To Our American Friends' read the large sign greeting Allison's team, code-named DEER, in Thai Nguyen, 75 miles north of Hanoi. Ragtag Vietminh guerrillas led Thomas to a small bamboo hut, where Ho Chi Minh confirmed the Chinese agent's information. In a later meeting, Ho pointed to the disguised Frenchman: 'This man is not an American.' After Thomas insisted he was, Ho correctly identified the man as Lieutenant Montfort of the French Army. Deeply impressed by the accuracy and scope of Ho's intelligence, including information on Japanese Army order of battle and troop movements, Thomas reported that the Vietminh deserved Allied support for commando operations.

After Ho volunteered a thousand 'well-trained' guerrillas for anti-Japanese operations, OSS-Kunming agreed to provide arms and training. The DEER Team adopted guerrilla garb, ate Vietnamese rice and remained in Ho's lair for over two months. The Americans trained 200 of Giap's élite troops in the latest commando tactics and replaced the guerrillas' antique firearms and knives with modern submachine guns, mortars and bazookas.

At the Big Three Conference at Potsdam in July 1945, an Anglo-American dispute over theater boundaries between the British Southeast Asia command and the American-led China theater was settled by dividing Indochina at the 16th parallel. Four Kuomintang armies would accept Japanese surrender in North Vietnam, while British troops under Lord Admiral Mountbatten would occupy the south. But VJ Day in Indochina saw Ho Chi Minh's guerrillas poised to fill the power vacuum created by Japan's collapse. Vietminh guerrillas marched on Hanoi in mid-August, reaping a groundswell of nationalist support. Vietminh

membership ballooned: even the French-trained and -armed Vietnamese militia joined in. Within 10 days, Hanoi was under the control of Vietminh militiamen, who occupied key government buildings. Vietminh shadow governments, 'People's Revolutionary Committees,' quickly popped up in Tonkinese villages, ousting pro-Japanese government officials. It would be almost a month before the first of 150,000 Chinese soldiers occupied northern Vietnam. The first Allied force into Hanoi arrived on 22 August: a 12-man OSS unit under Major Archimedes Patti, the SO branch chief who had directed Operation COMORE and other operations from Kunming.

The mission of Patti's 'QUAIL' team was to seek the release of some of the 20,000 Allied POWs and French troops imprisoned in hundreds of Japanese camps from Manchuria to Indochina. In July 1945, OSS had designated a number of commando 'Mercy Teams' to parachute into Japanese POW camps prior to a formal Japanese surrender. Mercy teams' secondary responsibility was to collect intelligence on political warfare activities for the OSS. Patti was accompanied by several uniformed officers from Mission 5, led by Major Jean Sainteny.

The American and French officers arrived in Hanoi to find a city ablaze with red and gold Vietminh flags. Armed propaganda detachments controlled the streets while self-defense militia armed with an odd assortment of weapons – modern Japanese rifles, old French hunting guns and flintlocks – roamed everywhere else. Patti's team watched as pro-Vietminh masses marched through the city, seizing the city armory and disarming Bao Dai's pro-Japanese militia without a shot.

The Vietnamese crowds welcomed the Americans warmly, but were openly hostile to the French. The Vietminh Provisional Government immediately placed Sainteny and his officers in 'protective custody' in the French Governor General's palace. OSS officers noted the general anti-French sentiment among the Vietnamese, and the deep fear among Hanoi's French population, who were subject to indiscriminate arrest and whose homes were being

Right: Vietnamese soldiers survey a collection of captured French weapons with evident satisfaction.

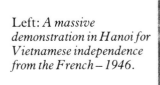

Left: A massive demonstration in Hanoi for Vietnamese independence from the French – 1946.

looted by armed Vietnamese bands. French officials pressed the Americans to arrange for release and rearmament of 4500 Frenchmen and Legionnaires imprisoned in the old Citadel, Hanoi's filthy and unsanitary prison. (Another generation of Americans would experience the Citadel's accommodations first-hand, and rename this same prison the 'Hanoi Hilton.') But OSS officials feared that release and rearming of Legionnaires might lead to a violent clash with thousands of now-armed Vietnamese. OSS actions, perceived by the French as constituting an anti-colonial, pro-Vietminh bias, earned the OSS lasting enmity among French officials. The Americans were, however, able to improve sanitary conditions at the Citadel.

The Vietminh takeover of Hanoi was complete by the end of August. Emperor Bao Dai abdicated in Hué on 30 August, paving the way for establishment of a Vietminh provisional government. Giap's elite OSS-trained guerrillas marched into Hanoi in a victory parade, accompanied by Captain Thomas and his team, reviewed by Ho Chi Minh and Major Patti. That same day, 1 September 1945, Ho Chi Minh proclaimed Vietnamese independence.

Major Patti reported to OSS-Kunming: 'Political situation here is critical.... Vietminh strong and belligerent and definitely anti-French. Suggest no more French be permitted to enter French Indochina and especially not armed.' General Lu Han's Chinese Nationalist troops arrived in mid-September, definitely not on any mission of mercy; Lu Han ignored American and French suggestions to disarm the Vietminh, and only grudgingly released French POWs from the Citadel. His Kuomintang troops not only took up positions in the Red River Delta, according to the Potsdam plan, but occupied the Laotian highlands as well, although no Japanese troops had been billeted there. The reason for this strategic deployment became clear with the arrival of the 1945 opium poppy harvest. The 93rd Kuomintang Army grabbed the entire crop and would refuse to withdraw until September 1946, after that year's harvest. It was not the last time that opium would play a major role in deployment of troops in Southeast Asia.

Although Lu Han finally allowed French troops to return late in 1946, Ho was able to pay off the general to allow a degree of Vietminh political autonomy at the expense of non-communist nationalists.

Although Ho Chi Minh remained master of his own destiny in Tonkin, his Vietminh was not nearly as strong farther south in Cochin China. Here the Vietminh faced numerous rival political and armed paramilitary groups, with each group vying either for outright power or at least for a way to carve out its own regional hegemony.

The best Vietminh political organization in the South was under the Vanguard Youth, *Thanh Nien Tien Phong*, a group reminiscent of a Boy Scout organization, complete with uniforms, songs and a strong nationalist orientation. Reported membership by 1945 was more than 200,000. Within the Vanguard Youth's leadership, however, was a clandestine cadre of dedicated communists, led by Pham Ngoc Thach. But Thach could not guarantee the same rigid discipline as the Tonkinese Vietminh.

OSS Southeast Asia command in Ceylon dis-

patched an intelligence team, code-named 'Embankment,' into southern Vietnam to operate as another mercy team. They were to locate Allied POWs and supervise their evacuation, but also to seize or microfilm Japanese documents and codebooks and track Japanese war criminals. The OSS teams, composed of both French- and Vietnamese-speaking officers, would also report on political trends – without revealing to the French the true nature of their mission.

The OSS 'Embankment' team was commanded by Major Peter Dewey, the son of a Republican Congressman who was a close friend of OSS Chief General William 'Wild Bill' Donovan. Dewey had been a journalist for the *Chicago Daily News* in Paris when the war broke out. While reporting on the war in 1940, he joined the Polish Army fighting the German invasion of France. He escaped through Portugal and ultimately joined the OSS. Fluent in French, Dewey had also parachuted into occupied France on OSS special operations.

Dewey's seven-man team arrived in Saigon in

Left: *Bao Dai, hereditary emperor of Annam and the French choice for ruler of Vietnam.*

early September, after a Provisional Executive Committee for the South composed of all major nationalist groups had seized control of Saigon from the Japanese. Vietnamese enthusiastically greeted the Embankment team, who quickly freed some 200 American POWs and arranged for their evacuation by C-47s. The team then proceeded, according to their orders, 'to represent American interests' and observe the political pressure-cooker that postwar Saigon would soon become.

The first of some 20,000 British Gurkhas of the 20th Indian Army, under command of British General Sir Douglas Gracey, arrived in Saigon on 13 September. The Gurkhas added still more color to

the panorama of Japanese, Americans, British, Vietnamese and French spilling through the streets. Gracey's orders were to restrict his actions to disarming Imperial Japanese Army troops.

Members of the Vietnamese Committee of the South, the *de facto* government of Cochin China, sought a meeting with General Gracey, who was unimpressed by the fledgling Vietnamese politicians. They 'came to see me and said "Welcome" and all that sort of thing,' Gracey remembered. 'It was an unpleasant situation and I promptly kicked them out.'

Gracey then demanded the disarming of all Vietminh, and gave the local Japanese commander

General LeClerc's troops embark for Indochina at Marseilles in September 1945. Some 250,000 French troops would be deployed in Southeast Asia during the following decade.

23

responsibility for pacifying the Vietnamese. In retaliation, Vietnamese nationalists called a general strike on 17 August. Gracey declared martial law on 21 September, imposed press censorship and banned all public demonstrations. He also released and rearmed some 1400 interned French soldiers – an act which rapidly eroded public order. The local French population took their cue from their compatriots, joining ragged and vengeful French soldiers in ousting the Vietnamese and reoccupying public buildings; street beatings and shootings of Vietnamese ensued, setting the stage for even greater violence.

The situation did not improve with the arrival of a well-armed French expeditionary corps of three full divisions and elite French naval airborne commandos. Led by General LeClerc, the 'liberator of Paris,' the fresh crack troops appeared formidable in their crisp new American khakis; they looked so GI-issue that it was difficult to distinguish American from French troops.

Appalled at the general breakdown in civil order

and what he considered General Gracey's reckless handling of the situation, Major Dewey openly criticized the British commander. The outraged Gracey did not take this criticism well, declaring the American major *persona non grata* and ordering him to leave Saigon within 24 hours.

Despite calls by the Committee of the South for public calm, some Vietnamese sought revenge against any Frenchman. Sniper fire broke out in the streets and roadblocks went up along major arteries on 25 September. That evening, about 150 French and Eurasian men and children were massacred by a renegade band of Binh Xuyen gangsters, and in a separate attack, OSS Captain Joseph Coolidge was seriously wounded in a Vietminh ambush. On 26 September, shortly before he was to depart for Ceylon, Major Dewey and another OSS officer riding in an open, unmarked jeep approached a Vietnamese roadblock near Saigon. Dewey, still angry at the wounding of Captain Coolidge, cursed the Vietnamese in perfect French as the jeep careened around the barricade. Shots rang out,

Top left: *British and French troops clearing the Saigon Triangle in the fall of 1945.*
Above: *The Citadel, Hanoi, where French prisoners lived under squalid conditions during World War II.*
Right: *Vietnamese prisoners taken near Saigon, during the civil disorder that erupted with the return of the French.*

instantly killing Dewey. Although he had been mistaken for a French officer, Dewey's was the first American death in the Vietnam war.

Amid escalating violence, the OSS teams withdrew from Indochina in late October. In one of its final reports, the Embankment team observed that Vietnamese hope that Americans were 'representatives of a new future' was fading. In December 1945, the British began evacuating the Gurkhas with the arrival of large numbers of French troops.

The *Deuxieme Bureau*, the scourge of Vietnamese nationalism, began to re-exert itself, but it was only a shadow of its prewar self in power and influence. Four years of war had destroyed French intelligence networks. Communists and nationalists alike were armed and organized as never before.

In the south, after the French *coup* of 23 September, most Vietminh leaders fled Saigon for the countryside to join their political enemies – Cao Dai, Hoa Hao, Binh Xuyen and other nationalist groups – in guerrilla resistance. In a matter of days, the French takeover had united all southerners.

The French-Vietminh War: 1946-54

Previous pages: *French paratroopers descend on Dienbienphu in Operation Castor, the prelude to the 56-day siege that broke France's hold on Indochina.*

The year 1946 started with the hope of a negotiated peace, but ended in violence. After the Vietminh won a clear majority in the National Assembly elections, it was obvious that France would have to negotiate with, or fight, the Democratic Republic of Vietnam, and its new president, Ho Chi Minh.

But the French were also dealing with the Kuomintang generals, signing away prewar territorial claims to China. The February 1946 Sino-French agreement paved the way for a Kuomintang withdrawal and a return of French military power to Tonkin.

Return of the French Army

Promising negotiations held in Paris between Ho and Jean Sainteny in March 1946 considered the prospect of Vietminh control over Tonkin and phase-out of French Government in Annam and Cochin China within France's Indochinese Federation. But Admiral Georges Thierry d'Argenlieu, the French High Commissioner, ordered returning French forces to continue their 'pacification' efforts in the south to wipe out Vietminh influence in these two 'French' regions.

In Tonkin, Giap quietly consolidated and prepared for war. As the last Kuomintang warlords stole back to China with their opium crop in September, he quickly neutralized and disarmed all pro-Chinese and non-communist militia. He with-

drew 38,000 troops into the rugged Viet Bac, scattered other units in small groups throughout the countryside and accepted covert military aid and advisers, smuggled by sea from Shanghai, from Mao Tse-tung's Chinese Communists. In October 1946, Ho returned from stalemated talks in Paris to find 60,000 Vietminh troops prepared for an inevitable showdown with the French.

It was not long in coming. A French patrol boat's seizure of an arms-laden Chinese junk in November led to a French ultimatum for Vietminh disarmament, sporadic street fighting and a brutal French reprisal. French cruisers and artillery lobbed heavy shells into Haiphong's residential areas on 23 November, killing an estimated 6000 Vietnamese.

Giap's opening move came on 19 December. Sappers from a 2000-man Vietminh rear guard blew up Hanoi's electric power station, ambushed French soldiers and mined city streets. After fierce house-to-house fighting with French troops, most of the rearguard guerrillas escaped the city via a secret underground tunnel.

Once again the French controlled Hanoi. But an American consul in Hanoi, weighing the new military balance in Indochina, cabled Washington that the guerrillas could fight on indefinitely.

Between 1945 and 1954, the French deployed over 250,000 French Union Forces, plus another 100,000 soldiers of the national armies of the 'Associated States' (Laos, Cambodia and Vietnam),

Below: *French Foreign Legionnaires in Saigon, February 1947.*
Opposite: *Paratroopers of the French Foreign Legion awaiting transport by the Red River Bridge near Hanoi, on their return from a patrol in 1951.*

to defeat the Vietminh. French nationals within all French Union units numbered only 55,000, although these men – including many St Cyr graduates – filled the key command cadre and headquarter staff positions.

Fighting to defeat communism and to restore French honor after the 1940 debacle, the French Army contained a colorful and truly international expeditionary corps ranging from the bearded, khaki-clad Foreign Legionnaires in white kepis to North African and Senegalese *spahis* in brightly colored cummerbunds. Other elements included assorted paramilitary forces of varying distinctions.

The bulk of the French expeditionary corps, composed entirely of volunteers, consisted of colonials – Moroccan, Algerian and Tunisian rifle regiments. Another third were native Indochinese serving in colonial army units (as opposed to the drab, conscripted 'national armies'). Many of these native Indochinese had previously served France with honor on various World War II battlefields.

The famed Foreign Legion comprised less than a quarter of the French Union forces, about 20,000 crack troops. Among the world's foremost soldiers of fortune, these professional mercenaries included some 7000 displaced European nationals. Although postwar French citizens disdained military service, the Legion found no shortage of volunteers among displaced Germans, Czechs or others fleeing Soviet-occupied Eastern Europe. The Legion also quietly recruited in German POW camps within the French occupation zones – a ready source of experienced and elite SS soldiers eager to fight communism.

Except for a few naval and airborne commando units, French occupation troops in Indochina displayed a rigid conventional cast. French military strategy to defeat the Vietminh guerrillas rested heavily upon crack Legionnaires and 'paras,' the elite paratrooper units. Most other French colonial units were organized and equipped to quell local insurrections, consisting of light combat units – infantry regiments and light armored cavalry, a few artillery battalions – of the type employed for static defense and pacification duties. French disdain for Giap's ragged, relatively poorly armed soldiers was evident in the failure to plan for an extended campaign against the Vietminh. Even elite forces retained little combat support and logistics for sustained field operations.

The French planned to employ their mobile forces in a lightning blow to crush Giap's troops, then mop up with colonial gendarme units. This strategy relied heavily on World War II conventional tactics and weapons proven on the plains of Europe – rapid pincer movements, mobile armored thrusts, paratroop envelopments and massed artillery – to repel expected Vietminh frontal attacks in set-piece battles.

The French high command hoped to wipe out the Vietminh insurgency in a single bold stroke. To capture top Vietminh leaders inside their jungle hideouts, the French launched an ambitious plan code-named Operation LEA in October 1947. LEA combined paratroop drops and deep armored thrusts by 15,000 men in 20 battalions into a 100-square-mile triangle of Tonkin's most inaccessable terrain. Nearly 1200 paratroopers storming Ho Chi Minh's Viet Bac headquarters achieved tactical surprise. They found Ho's worktable, complete with papers ready for signature, and captured vast stores of arms, food and matériel. However, in a defensive maneuver often repeated, Ho's entire top command and 40,000 Vietminh slipped through the French pincer movement and into the jungle. Thus began the French military's search for a conventional set-piece battle against Ho's elusive guerrillas.

Right: *The postwar Franco-Vietnamese Conference at Fontainbleau.*
Far right: *European residents of Hanoi welcome returning French troops.*

Residents of Hanoi rally for Vietnamese independence in March 1946; the speaker urges support for the Nationalist movement led by Ho Chi Minh.

'The Front Was Nowhere; It Was Everywhere'

Although the rhetoric behind Ho Chi Minh's concept of people's warfare borrowed heavily from Mao Tse-tung, it also drew upon a long Vietnamese tradition of protracted conflict against incomparably superior enemies. His major contribution to traditional Vietnamese guerrilla warfare was organization. Ho skillfully motivated his followers through discipline, indoctrination and ideological fervor – disguised as nationalism. His quasi-religious doctrine of *dau tranh*, or struggle, molded the Vietminh into a strongly disciplined force with an iron will to drive out the hated French colonialists. The Vietnamese tiger, Ho had predicted, would allow the French elephant no respite.

Giap's military strategy was also vintage Mao, adapted to a Vietnamese context. His revolutionary warfare doctrine contained three distinct phases. In the earliest phase, guerrilla tactics were employed in defensive actions, while insurgents established firm control of, and support from, the rural population. During the next phase, main force units were formed within the revolutionary base and offensive operations started against isolated and immobile enemy outposts. In a climactic final phase, guerrilla main forces, aided by a popular 'general uprising,' would overwhelm remaining enemy forces and achieve final victory. (Although the projected general uprising never took place, the victory did.)

Giap's guerrilla army had a pyramid-like struc-

ture organized into three types of military units. The lowest and broadest level contained the guerrilla-militia forces (*dan quan* and *dan quan du kich*). The true foundation of people's warfare, these part-time guerrillas were found at the hamlet and village level and served as the principal means of enlisting the total population in the communist cause. The 30–50-man guerrilla-militia platoons were poorly armed, with perhaps a handful of bolt-action rifles, homemade hand grenades, or even some spears and knives. Like their weapons, their training was rudimentary, but the *dan quan* mission was crucial to the Vietminh attrition strategy: to act as a 'home guard,' conduct local patrols to monitor and harass French military movements, engage in sabotage. This mission included preparation of local defenses – the mines, punji stakes and booby traps that claimed the majority of French casualties.

Better-armed *dan quan du kich* performed as local 'elite irregulars,' often taking part in actions outside the village, such as armed propaganda in neighboring areas, or protecting the village Communist Party apparatus. These units also served as a manpower pool for larger regional forces. Overall, guerrilla-militia units numbered over 100,000 by 1954; they existed in thousands of hamlets from the Ca Mau Peninsula in the south to the Chinese border.

The second-largest level consisted of regional forces (*dia phong*) organized into 85-man district-level companies and 300-man province battalions. District companies comprised local strike forces to support village militias, assist province battalions, or protect the district party command and control apparatus. Province battalions were organized along more conventional lines (although always operating within prevailing guerrilla doctrine), with several rifle companies and a weapons-support company with light machine guns and sometimes mortars. When fully equipped, regional units could engage equal-sized French Union forces in sustained combat for short periods. Regional units – some 70,000 by 1954 – also served as a general reserve for main force units (*chu luc*). These highly mobile 400-man light infantry battalions constituted the Vietminh's major offensive strike forces.

During the initial defensive phase of people's war, the Vietminh focused on expanding the Viet Bac, where Giap's guerrillas honed their fighting skills to break the 'initial dash' of the French expeditionary corps. Supplementing the 4600 small arms dropped by the OSS, and several thousand captured French and Japanese rifles, were crude jungle arms factories that manufactured their own guns and ammunition.

To guard against French incursions into the Viet Bac, where Giap was building his main force units, regional and guerrilla-militia troops occasionally conducted armed forays against isolated French garrisons, often spearheaded by special *kamikaze*-like units known as 'volunteers of death' that infiltrated and blew open French defenses to be followed by swarming infantry.

However, the chief military function of guerrilla-militia and regional forces was to consolidate their hold on rural populations and to pin down French military forces. Insurgents emphasized small-unit actions – sabotage, harassing actions and ambush – to force the French high command to disperse scarce

troops countrywide to protect vulnerable targets.

Steady attrition inflicted by Vietminh auxiliaries wore down French morale and finally put French Union forces on the defensive. By 1948 French offensive actions focused on three kinds of restrictive operation: pacification, protection of convoys and mobile thrusts against the Viet Bac revolutionary base (steadily decreasing in frequency.) Although French colonial units appeared well suited for pacification operations, such missions used up scarce manpower and failed to eradicate the Vietminh infrastructure. Attempts to repeat the success of earlier, prewar Foreign Legion 'oil spot' techniques proved unsuccessful against *dan quan* and *dia phong* irregulars. Colonial units often succeeded in chasing out larger, more conspicuous, Vietminh companies or battalions, but remained oblivious to the omnipresent underground platoons that set booby traps and harassed colonial troops. Ostensibly 'cleared' areas were, in fact, never free from organized, disciplined guerrilla activity. Pacification became a war with no clearly defined front. 'The front was nowhere,' Giap wrote later, 'it was everywhere.'

Such lightning thrusts as Operation LEA proved equally costly in terms of human casualties, but took a greater toll on precious and expensive aircraft, armor and artillery. Combined operations were especially hard on the elite paras. Operation LEA had cost 1000 lives and 3000 wounded. Convoy operations – necessary to resupply the chain of forts and French border posts – played into Vietminh strengths while draining French troops from other operations. The roadside ambush is an age-old

Soldiers of the Nationalist Chinese Army seek refuge in a French camp in Indochina, where they receive vaccinations (1950).

Main picture: *French
parachutists on the Plain of
Joncs, around Biong Dinh.*
Inset: *Moroccan troops
fighting for France in
Indochina – 1947.*

French gunners on the alert at Mao Khe, where a small garrison repulsed 21 Vietminh battalions with the help of American weapons and supplies.

guerrilla tactic in which the Vietminh excelled. Sometimes the Vietminh would employ several battalions at a single chokepoint to pounce on a 200-vehicle French convoy. Large convoys required up to five infantry battalions with mobile artillery support.

A favorite Vietminh trick, one to which French (and later American) commanders would frequently succumb, was the tactic 'Assail the fort and strike the rescuers,' used with great success in Giap's first major offensive in 1948 against mud and bamboo French forts along Colonial Route 4. For Foreign Legionnaires of the 3rd Regiment on the Sino-Vietnamese border, it was only a question of time before the communists siezed the initiative. Vietminh

harassing attacks on French convoys and outposts made border duty unpleasant. Old-timers grumbled that Tonkin duty was nothing like the free-wheeling prewar days. They complained that even their *choum* (rice wine) and *congai*, the beautiful Vietnamese women, had changed – perhaps because the French high command warned that the Vietminh were poisoning the wine and infecting the *congai* with venereal disease.

The situation got far worse at Phu Tong Hoa near Cao Bang on 25 July 1948. Quietly infiltrating the scrub-brush hill near the Legion post, 4000 Vietminh attacked with hurricane force to the screams of *Tien len!* (Forward!) The Legionnaires survived only by their fingernails – at a frightful cost. While

the Vietminh failed to overrun the post, the attack tested Giap's blood-curdling 'human-wave' tactic and gave the Legion a taste of what was to come. Stepped-up attacks on convoys continued to the point where the Legion was losing more men on convoys than in the posts they were supposed to relieve. RC 4 quickly developed a reputation as a hot zone. 'Ah, you're not married,' grizzled veterans would joke at young replacements in Hanoi: 'Good! You're for RC 4, where bachelors can die without too much family fuss.'

However, Giap's 1948 border campaign was only a rehearsal for the curtain-raiser the following year, when Mao Tse-tung's decisive victory over Chiang Kai-shek's once-mighty Kuomintang tipped the strategic balance in Indochina in the Vietminh's favor. As Mao's Red Army occupied southern China, Giap received a wealth of new military equipment – American arms captured from the Kuomintang – for his main forces. In addition to the supplies, 15,000 Communist Chinese advisors flowed over the border of Kwangsi Province and by

sea from the Chinese-controlled island of Hainan.

In a single month, French intelligence estimated that the Vietminh received 50,000 rifles, 150 Browning automatic rifles (BARs), 95 machine guns, 30 mortars and numerous 75- and 130mm guns. Giap's troops received some weapons, including the versatile US-made recoilless rifle, even before the French, giving the communists an edge in light, mobile firepower necessary for jungle fighting. Heavier weapons meant larger, better-equipped formations, standardized arms, improved transport and communication lines from China. Main forces could both initiate and sustain larger operations, breaking the pre-1949 stalemate. Giap moved immediately to widen the Chinese logistical pipeline by targeting isolated French forts along the Chinese frontier.

Rapid cross-country mobility allowed Vietminh main forces to choose the time and place for battle. Without credible intelligence on Vietminh movements in rural areas, the French high command often underestimated Giap's ability to shuttle his

The flag of Ho Chi Minh flies over a revolutionary outpost discovered by French soldiers near Thai Nguyen.

Some 30,000 Chinese Nationalists fled across the border into Vietnam to escape advancing Chinese Communist forces in 1950. They were interned at a huge camp on Phu Quoc Island, where residents seen here cheer a visit by Wing Fong-tsao, the Nationalist Chinese representative in Saigon.

forces on the battlefield. Lacking mechanical transport and shunning the roads for fear of French fighter aircraft, Vietminh main forces excelled in fast cross-country movement. Camouflaged by thick jungle canopies, these groups traveled light and fast in smaller units, concentrating rapidly prior to attack.

In September 1950, Giap massed 14 infantry and 3 artillery battalions and began rolling up French border posts. Communist troops quickly overran Dong Khe, then attacked and destroyed a major French convoy near Cao Bang. For the first time, well-disciplined Vietminh troops chopped up French units in open combat. Panic-stricken French soldiers hastily evacuated Lang Son, the key French position on the Chinese frontier, abandoning 13 artillery pieces, 125 mortars, 450 trucks, over 900 machine guns and 9000-plus rifles and submachine guns – enough matériel to equip an entire Vietminh division.

The French lost over 6000 troops. A few hundred disorganized stragglers fell back on Hanoi, spreading panic in French civilian and military circles. Vietminh Radio, in a textbook display of psychological warfare, encouraged the hysteria. In Hanoi and Haiphong, French civilians and military alike were gripped in what one French officer described as 'a pychosis of fear,' prompting some military officers to arrange for evacuation of their dependents.

American observers commented that the Sino-Vietnamese frontier 'had ceased to exist.' By New Year's Day of 1951, the French had lost control of all of Vietnam north of the Red River. The key road to Hanoi – into the populous Red River Delta – was wide open.

Vietminh on the Strategic Offensive

Appointment of General Jean de Lattre de Tassigny as the new French commander-in-chief in 1951 provided a much-needed boost for French morale. General de Lattre was a popular and romantic figure in France, the youngest general in the French Army in 1940 and the one who had led the 1st French Army in its drive to the Rhine in 1944, restoring national pride after the debacle of 1940. The general stepped off the plane in Hanoi in full dress uniform, brimming with confidence and *élan*. 'I am proud to again find myself at the head of a French army in battle,' the dashing de Lattre announced. 'From this point, soldiers of France, you will be led!'

De Lattre's brave display calmed the panic over the loss of Lang Son. The general canceled evacuation plans, installed his wife in Hanoi and embarked on an immediate inspection tour of the battlefield. He grasped quickly the strategic significance of loss of the border region: all major roads from China to the Viet Bac lay open. China itself became the 'large rear base,' a sanctuary for a steady flow of supplies. Eventually, Giap's main forces would challenge French military control of the rich Red River Delta.

The military situation forced de Lattre to re-examine French strategy and tactics in light of Vietminh gains. Communist control over the frontier enabled Giap to fight a long war, reducing the contest to a test of French political will. De Lattre's task was to regain the military initiative to demonstrate that will. His first priority was to secure the tenuous French hold on the Delta and seal it off from Vietminh political activities. Arrival of French reinforcements – an armored regiment, anti-aircraft regiment, parachute battalion, two artillery battalions and five battalions of North African and Senegalese infantry – in late 1950 shored up French positions in Tonkin. Fortification of the 'de Lattre Line' was designed to deny the Vietminh military manpower while the French recruited and trained an able Vietnamese National Army. This native army would then free up French Union forces to regain the strategic initiative in Tonkin.

In response to rapid mobility of the Vietminh foot soldier, de Lattre reorganized French forces to optimize available military resources and adapt to local conditions and Vietminh tactics. The general established mobile reserves called *groupe mobiles* to react to anticipated Vietminh offensive operations. These were composite units, resembling US regimental combat teams, composed of tanks, mechanized infantry, armored scout cars, self-propelled artillery and commandos – shock-troop units used for reconnaissance. The self-contained *groupe mobile*, was, as historian Bernard Fall observed, 'an ever-moving microcosm of an army,' capable of tremendous firepower.

Other tactical changes included establishment of *dinassauts*, naval assault divisions. Resembling a flotilla of American Civil War-era 'monitors,' French *dinassauts* included surplus US landing craft of various types, locally modified with armor plates, tank turrets and artillery pieces for added firepower. They were designed to project French firepower and support operations into Indochina's thousands of miles of navigable rivers, where vulnerable French convoys dared not venture.

The average *dinassaut* consisted of a dozen rivercraft including an armored LSSL (Landing Ship Support, Large) as flagship, several other LCM (Landing Craft, Matériel) 'monitors' as fire support and six other LCMs carrying either 81mm mortars, supplies, or two companies of French marine commandos. Larger *dinassauts* of up to 20 ships included LCTs (Landing Craft, Tanks) that carried tanks, artillery, troops, even reconnaissance aircraft, hundreds of miles upriver into battle zones. Six *dinassauts* were eventually deployed in Indochina, four in the southern Mekong Delta and two in Tonkin.

Dinassauts and *groupe mobiles* represented a French trend toward unconventional formations, equipment and tactical employment under de Lattre's command. Their *ad hoc* development revealed a critical French military weakness obvious to Giap: the need to safeguard vulnerable lines of communications while simultaneously forcing Vietminh battalions into open battle, where French firepower was most effective. De Lattre's innovations were a tacit recognition that previous conventional French doctrine – based on World War II lessons learned on European battlefields – was inadequate both to Indochinese terrain and to Ho Chi Minh's concept of revolutionary warfare.

Ironically, as de Lattre developed unconventional mobile units to draw Vietminh main forces into a pitched battle, General Giap prepared for a climactic 'general counteroffensive' in the Red River Delta in 1951. Massive Chinese aid had expanded the Vietminh main force from a few battalions and regi-

ments into full divisions. By 1950 Giap had formed five new divisions – the 304th, 308th, 312th, 316th, 320th – in Tonkin and the 325th in Annam (central Vietnam). Giap later created the 351st 'heavy' division – two artillery regiments and one of engineers – based on the Soviet pattern. In January 1951, flushed with his success at Lang Son, Giap launched a massive offensive with 81 battalions.

Giap's premature 'counteroffensive' played directly into de Lattre's strength – the tremendous firepower of mobile groups and *dinassauts* plus French air superiority. This was exactly the type of battle for which de Lattre had prepared his troops. In January Giap sent two divisions against two mobile groups defending Vin Yen, a small town northwest of Hanoi. In four days of intense fighting, Giap committed 21 main-force battalions, including 'human-wave' infantry assaults, against concentrated French tank and artillery positions.

French fighters, employing US-made napalm for the first time in Indochina, pounded exposed Vietminh troops. The newly formed Mobile Groups 1

Top: *A Moroccan unit fights the 'village war' in Tonkin in 1950. Six Tonkin provinces were overrun by Vietminh forces during World War II.* Above: *One hundred thousand soldiers of the Associated States of Laos, Cambodia and Vietnam fought with French forces to defeat the Vietminh between 1945-54. Here, a Legionnaire carries a wounded Vietnamese comrade.*

and 2 beat back repeated assaults. The Vietminh withdrew on 17 January, leaving behind 1500 dead and over 500 prisoners. French attempts to counter-attack were aborted by heavy casualties on their part. Mobile Group 2, comprised of two Moroccan and one para battalion totaling about 2000 men, suffered almost 540 casualties.

In March Giap struck again, at the Mao Khe garrison, which was outnumbered three to one. Aided by now-generous supplies of American war matériel, and enjoying clear superiority in artillery and air support, six French battalions repulsed another 21-battalion Vietminh assault. Again, casualties on both sides were heavy: 1200 Vietminh dead left on the battlefield, another 500 Vietminh prisoners, three French battalions severely depleted.

A final, desperate Vietminh assault came in the delta plains of the Day River in June 1951. A division-sized Vietminh attack fell on the Catholic town of Ninh Binh, defended by a small French garrison but supported by the 3rd *Dinassaut* and its 80 marine commandos. General de Lattre's son, Lt Bernard de Lattre, and over 60 commandos died holding off the communists until reinforced by three mobile groups, the elite 7th Colonial Parachute Battalion and 105mm artillery units. With clear fields of fire in the open delta, French artillery tore large gaps in Vietminh ranks.

Giap ordered a withdrawal on 10 June. North Vietnam's top military strategist would long remember the tactical lessons of his aborted Red River

offensive. His postmortems of the 1951 offensive stressed the need for tactical flexibility and continued co-ordination among the three types of military forces – main forces, regional guerrillas and local militia. Never again would Giap deliberately fight the battle for which his enemy had prepared.

After the 1951 Delta battles, de Lattre sought to apply the same tactical concepts offensively against the Vietminh, while Giap refocused on more traditional guerrilla tactics. Late in 1951 his guerrillas began to penetrate the strategic T'ai mountain country between Hanoi and Laos, populated by various ethnic tribes organized by the French into irregular mountaineer companies. Since French Union forces had been stretched to their limits in more populated areas, these T'ai partisans, or *suppletifs*, were all that stood between Giap's main forces and the conquest of Laos.

French high command in Hanoi tried to divert Giap's attention by seizing Hoa-Binh, a major Vietminh supply center on the Black River, in a November 1951 airborne assault. Two thousand paras of the 1st, 2nd and 7th Colonial Parachute Battalions jumped into Hoa-Binh. Fifteen infantry and seven artillery battalions, backed by two armored groups and two *dinassauts*, followed the paras into the area. Giap refused the French challenge to another set-piece battle. Instead, the Vietminh encircled Hoa-Binh.

During the Hoa-Binh campaign, the nimble and brave Vietminh foot soldier exhibited the tactics for which he became famous. Vietminh assaults were

A B-26 on the airstrip at the French garrison of Cat-Bi: 15 March 1951

carefully prepared and practiced, often requiring pre-positioned stores and sometimes months of re-hearsals by assault troops using maps of scale-model sand tables. Against fixed French positions, com-munist troops often resorted to human-wave attacks, a costly but effective tactic that rattled French Union defenders. Such an attack began with the shrill screams of *Tien Len!*, heralding a first wave of grenadiers armed mainly with hand grenades, followed by frenzied massed infantry. Isolation of Hoa-Binh included a human-wave assault against the French outpost at Tu-Vu in December 1951. Five Vietminh battalions threw themselves against 200 Moroccan riflemen and a supporting tank platoon. In fierce close-quarter combat, US-made M-24 light tanks fired at minimum elevation into the sea of Communist infantry. Although they killed scores of Vietminh, the Moroccan tankers were soon engulfed by the swarming guerrillas, who fired Tommy guns and dropped incendiary grenades into crew slits. Trapped crews were roasted alive and surviving riflemen driven into the Black River.

Vietminh troops also relied on more orthodox guerrilla tactics like surprise and stealth. Isolated Foreign Legion units were often picked as the mark. At Xon-Pheo outside Hoa-Binh, in January 1952, a clever Vietminh sapper unit stalked a returning patrol of the Foreign Legion's 13th Demi-Brigade through a Legionnaire minefield, then quickly blew carefully prepared defenses with TNT charges and bangalore torpedoes. Only a brave bayonet charge in classic Legion tradition prevented the Vietminh from completely overrunning the compound and cutting the main road to Hanoi, Colonial Route 6.

The battle hinged on control of the Black River at Hoa-Binh salient. From December through January, French *dinassauts* patroled hundreds of miles up the Black River in one of the bloodiest riverine battles since the American Civil War. French LCMs armed with tank turrets and quad .50-caliber machine guns dueled Vietminh shore batteries for control of the vital waterway. Vietminh gunners jerryrigged recoilless rifles and artillery from camouflaged shore points and used mines and even frogmen against the shallow-draft *dinassauts*.

When the French committed three mobile groups and an airborne group around Hoa-Binh, the Viet-minh refused combat and faded away. Shortly after the French investment of Hoa Binh, de Lattre was stricken with cancer; he died in 1952 after his return to Paris. With de Lattre's death, French initiative faltered. When the Vietminh succeeded in cutting the Black River and threatened to close Route 6, de Lattre's successor, General Raoul Salan, ordered the evacuation of Hoa-Binh. For the next six months, French mobile groups strained – with little success – to keep open the approaches to the T'ai hills. By late 1952, the strategic initiative belonged again to General Giap's Vietminh irregulars.

While French mobile units sought to lure the elusive Vietminh main-force units into battle a second time, local communist guerrillas throughout Vietnam worked at winning the 'village war,' a con-flict based not on big units or mobile tactics, but on a sophisticated form of subversive insurgent warfare in which Ho Chi Minh's forces excelled.

The key to Vietminh success would be uncondi-tional support from the population, secured in one of two ways: first by appealing to the peasants' latent nationalism, or failing that, by the selected use of terror. Normally, the first targets of communist terrorism were recalcitrant village leaders, petty government functionaries and those suspected of acting as regular French agents, providing intel-ligence on clandestine communist activities. Once the subversive and compartmentalized party organ-ization had gained the upper hand, the French found it nearly impossible to dislodge in the absence of a comparable intelligence network.

The loss of their prewar ability to penetrate sub-versive revolutionary groups forced the French to seek open warfare against Vietminh main-force units (a game Giap refused to play after his 1951 delta fiasco) or to rely on ineffective 'Pacification'

A group of Vietminh prisoners under guard after their capture by French troops in a Tonkin village; several of the communists had grenades concealed in their rice baskets.

The French garrison at Ninh Binh was almost overwhelmed by Vietminh troops before reinforcements arrived. General de Lattre's son, Lieutenant Bernard de Lattre, was killed in the fighting here (June 1951).

operations. The string of strong defensive positions in the delta, the so-called de Lattre Line, fared little better against clandestine Vietminh actions. The Vietminh high command, partially to divert French resources from Hoa-Binh, but also in line with people's warfare, infiltrated 25,000 guerrilla regulars into the Red River Delta region to recruit and train new regional and guerrilla-militia units.

Within months, over 30,000 Vietminh in 3 regular regiments, 14 regional battalions and 140 local *dan quan* militia companies became active inside the de Lattre line. These forces included the crack Vietminh 42nd Independent Regiment, an elite infantry unit permanently stationed in the Delta. Operating clandestinely, the 42nd Regiment survived all French attempts to annihilate it and remained in place at war's end. A total of 80,000 Vietminh guerrillas operated inside the de Lattre line by 1954. Their chief mission – besides tying down thousands of French troops – was to disrupt French transportation and lines of communication. When the French assigned an entire mobile group to guard the key Hanoi-Haiphong highway, Vietminh

guerrillas chopped the artery to pieces via mines, ambushes and blown bridges, and spied on French military movements. Communist saboteurs also engaged in covert activities inside the de Lattre line, with an impact far out of proportion to their small numbers. Due to Vietminh sabotage, an estimated 40 percent of French military equipment was delivered to front-line units with wrecked gears, torn or defective wiring, or ruined engines resulting from sugar poured into gas tanks.

The Tonkin village war was repeated in the Central Highlands and Mekong Delta regions. To challenge the Vietminh at the village level, the French enlisted a variety of anti-Vietminh paramilitary groups. In largely Catholic villages in Tonkin, the French recruited and armed nominally anti-French, but fiercely anti-communist, Catholic militias. Farther south, poorly armed Self-Defense Corps and Civil Guard militias operated as auxiliaries to the Vietnamese National Army, which was ill prepared for the difficult task of rooting out communist armed propaganda teams and cadres. Occasionally, industrious French officers working with local Vietnamese achieved some success. In one pacified province of 400,000 Vietnamese, French Army Colonel Leroy organized his own self-defense militia, supervised village councils and established his own intelligence network and economic program. But the success of such experiments varied with the resourcefulness of French officers.

Government militias were supplemented by paramilitary units of the *Cao Dai* and *Hoa Hao* religious sects and the *Binh Xuyen*. These traditionally anti-French forces had at various times co-operated with the Japanese and the Vietminh. But heavy-handed communist attempts to subvert and take over these groups led to a flimsy and unreliable coalition of French *suppletifs*.

The focus of de Lattre's long-range military strategy – the rapid training of an effective Vietnamese National Army – moved slowly. Although plans called for a 60,000-man army to replace French units in static pacification duty, fewer than 40,000 troops had been raised by early 1951, only 7 of whose 24 battalions were actually commanded by Vietnamese. Moreover, the conventional training these troops received proved inadequate either to counter the clandestine communist organizational structure in the villages or to meet disciplined Vietminh units in combat.

One French proposal to outfox the Vietminh at their own game generated enthusiasm from French legislators, who by 1951 had grown increasingly skeptical of military success. In expanding the Vietnamese Army, the French had planned for 52 special commando battalions, named *Tien-Doan Kinh-Quan* (TDKQ), to seek out local Vietminh regional and militia units on their own terrain. In theory, the TDKQ would flush local Vietminh units into the open, where destruction by heavier French forces awaited them. French legislators, weary of mounting casualties, believed that vast hordes of TDKQ commandos armed with Tommy guns would soon run roughshod over demoralized Vietminh irregulars.

The lightly armed 250-man TDKQ units were essentially light infantry battalions, well suited for the mission of village warfare, with its emphasis on unconventional tactics and knowledge of local terrain and politics. But public relations triumphed over patience. The French psychological warfare (psywar) office in Hanoi seized upon the TDKQ concept, hailing it as a 'secret weapon' against the communists. Vietminh commanders, either genuinely fearful of the TDKQ's combat potential or using their own psywar gambit, targeted the initial units for destruction by two main-force regiments inside the Red River Delta. In an unintended mismatch, these well-armed Vietminh units swiftly crushed the small, understrength TDKQ units, smashing both the psywar benefits and the 'secret weapon.' Embarrassment over the debacle led to the quiet demise of the promising TDKQ concept in 1954.

The French were far more successful at organizing the ethnic tribesmen in the highlands of Indochina – the Nung, Meo, T'ai, Muong and others with a traditional antipathy toward lowland Vietnamese. The French organized these fierce fighting men into *suppletif* and counterguerrilla units that harassed Vietminh base areas and supply lines led by

a few rugged French officers and irregulars. In Central Vietnam, the French-led *Garde Montagnard* (Mountaineer Guard) produced tough, aggressive soldiers, the best of whom were integrated into a composite battalion, the *Battaillon de Marche Indochinois* (BMI). Made up of Europeans, Cambodians and hardy *Montagnards*, the BMI was one of the best units in the French Union Forces, serving in many Indochinese hotspots like Hoa-Binh. Even 'le BEPs,' the tough Foreign Legion paratroop battalions, maintained a company of ethnic Indochinese in each unit to guide Legionnaires through unfamiliar territory.

When properly employed as irregulars, tribal partisans were extremely useful in reconnoitering rapid Vietminh movements through dense jungle. Occasionally, mountaineers helped save regular French units from complete annihilation by Vietminh main-force units, as when Giap renewed his drive into the T'ai highlands in October 1952. The 308th, 312th and 316th Vietminh Divisions moved in a three-pronged front against the weak French outposts west of the Red River and captured the strategic Nghia Lo ridges. French commanders felt it was impossible to hold the remaining outposts and assigned the crack 6th Colonial Parachute Battalion, commanded by Major Marcel Bigeard, to jump into Tu Le to fight a thankless rearguard action. Sacrifice of the paras allowed slower and larger French units to pull back toward the Delta.

Vietminh infantry, who expertly camouflaged their advances on Tu Le, surrounded Bigeard's command, cutting off the 6th Colonial Paratroopers' line of retreat. After the French, carrying their wounded, ran head-on into an ambush set by the 312th Vietminh Division, the small 284th Local *Suppletif* Company at Muong Chen offered to cover their escape. The 80 T'ai irregulars and 3 French NCOs at Muong Chen held off the Vietminh as Bigeard's paras escaped toward the safety of the

French Paratroops of the Second battalion prepare to leave Bach-May in January 1952.

Black River, 40 miles away. The battalion arrived two days later, two-fifths of its original strength.

The jungle-wise T'ai irregulars broke out themselves after battling the entire 213th Vietminh for several hours. Forty T'ai and French survivors escaped down narrow jungle paths known only to the partisans and led several Vietminh companies in a deadly game of hide-and-seek in the jungle for several days, carrying only weapons and ammo. By living off the land – eating manioc roots and corn-cobs – and by their wits, 16 survivors of the Muong Chen garrison eventually reached the Black River. But the partisans had played a crucial role in saving a major French unit and delaying the communist takeover of the highlands.

Other partisans covered the French retreat from the T'ai country. Commando Groups (GCs – *Groupement Commandos*) and Composite Airborne Commando Groups (GCMAs) had been organized by General de Lattre in 1951 in response to successful Vietminh guerrilla tactics. GC and GCMA partisans reported directly to French Central Intelligence in Hanoi.

Commando Groups used loyal native tribesmen as special counterguerrilla strike forces, often commanded by a native officer and French NCOs. GCs performed intelligence-gathering, reconnaissance and strike-force functions, and sometimes worked in close co-ordination with conventional French combat forces or native *suppletifs*.

GCMAs, on the other hand, functioned as guerrillas behind communist lines. Their mission was to form semiautonomous native *maquis* groups in the Vietminh's own backyard, collecting intelligence and harassing communist logistical lines. Over 20,000 GCMAs eventually operated between the rubber plantations north of Saigon and the Chinese border.

Command of the GCMAs fell to Major Roger Trinquier, an experienced Indochina hand. Like Vo Nguyen Giap, Trinquier was a schoolteacher drawn to the study of guerrilla warfare. During the 1930s, he served in the French Marine infantry in the Far East, commanding a remote outpost in one of the wildest sections on the Sino-Vietnamese frontier. While depending on local natives for assistance and information in fighting Chinese pirates and opium smugglers, the young officer learned many local mountaineer dialects.

Trinquier had seen combat in Vietnam twice before assuming the GCMA command; first in early 1946, as a platoon commander with the *Commando Ponchardier*, a French naval airborne commando unit, and in late 1947 as commander of the 1st Colonial Parachute Battalion. On both tours Trinquier had performed the tough duty of clearing Vietminh guerrillas out of the Plain of Reeds, personally leading his paras on four assaults into the swamp paddies outside Saigon. Because of the young officer's airborne commando training and his knowledge of the northern hills and tribes, General de Lattre chose Trinquier to implant anti-communist partisans deep inside the Vietminh stronghold.

A born irregular, Trinquier was critical of his army's conventional counterinsurgency methods. He later compared the French military machine to 'a pile driver attempting to crush a fly, indefatigably persisting in repeating its efforts' (a charge applicable also to conventional American tactics in the 1960s). Broad-scale combat operations and periodic commando raids, Trinquier argued, caused the communists only passing concern. Such operations were too brief and superficial – aimed at destroying recognizable main-force units rather than the clandestine Vietminh combat and intelligence organiza-

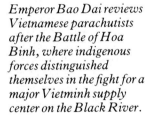

Emperor Bao Dai reviews Vietnamese parachutists after the Battle of Hoa Binh, where indigenous forces distinguished themselves in the fight for a major Vietminh supply center on the Black River.

tion. Messy anti-guerrilla operations of the type he had led, Trinquier believed, were also insufficient to defeat Giap's revolutionary warfare. Since the communist waged his war from an active sanctuary – whether populated village or mountian redoubt – the only effective response would be counter-infiltration of that sanctuary itself. Waging a guerrilla war on the Vietminh was contingent upon gaining the support of the local populace and several key factors: a 'specially adapted organization' with 'appropriate methods of warfare,' the firm intention to prevail and a considerable investment in time. A guerrilla *maquis* could not spring up overnight.

Contrary to the predictions of more conventionally minded French officers, the first GCMA contact teams that parachuted into enemy territory managed to fight and survive. Like the early Vietminh, GCMA actions like recruitment, assembly and training were conducted in absolute secrecy. The contact team's initial task was to carve out protected base areas – similar to Mao's Yenan caverns or Ho's Viet Bac. French NCOs recruited and trained 'specialized volunteer cadres,' the locals and Frenchmen who would later lead functioning *maquis* groups. The contact teams divided these cadres into three categories: about half served as combat personnel, a quarter as communications specialists and the rest as political and intelligence agents. To maximize secrecy, night airdrops by special French aircrews supplied the core group with equipment needed to recruit and train larger groups. Four to six months were required to establish a core group of about 10 trained contact teams within a selected *maquis* zone.

In the second phase, these contact teams began recruiting combat and intelligence units of about 300-400 men each. After several months of training, these units would begin to dismantle local Vietminh

administration, neutralize local police and security forces and establish the *maquis* group as the ultimate authority in the village. According to Trinquier, this sometimes required 'a few well-calculated acts of sabotage or terrorism' to compel any recalcitrant citizen to support the *maquis*.

Harassment of communications lines within the region served to isolate the *maquis* zone from Vietminh interference, allowing further development and extension of the GCMA force. The goal was to rapidly reach an effective weapons strength of 1000 rifles. Backed by 2000-3000 local villagers, some 1000 armed *maquisards* were considered sufficient to survive attacks by regional police and security units and, according to Trinquier, to 'create disturbances of incalculable magnitude in the enemy's country.'

GCMA units moved into the larger towns in the third phase to establish assembly and refuge areas,

Below: Communist soldiers exult on the wreck of a French B-26 brought down in 1951.
Bottom: A French Air Force plane overflies the scene of a 1951 bombing mission against Vietminh strongholds 100 miles north of Hanoi.

and perhaps build an 'airhead' for more reliable aerial resupply. GCMA agents also organized intelligence networks and caused outlying Vietminh-controlled villages further trouble. GCMA insurgents sought to recruit or convert Vietminh guerrillas and prisoners, in an attempt to sow mistrust among communist units.

Like Trinquier himself, French GCMA cadres who parachuted behind enemy lines were a special handpicked breed, usually chosen as much for their reputations among regular officers as 'trouble-makers' as for their command of strange dialects. GCMAs frequently 'went native,' sometimes even marrying into hill tribes in order to gain the trust and respect of the local village chieftain. Life for the French GCMa commando leader, dropped 200 miles from French lines, was difficult and extremely dangerous. The war in the hill country was a harsh, brutal struggle without quarter. The GCMA soldier had no future other than total victory or death; he had no hope of regular rotation or even quick evacuation if wounded. GCMA units carried their wounded with them; capture by the Vietminh meant certain torture and virtual suicide for that particular GCMA unit. The murderous climate and unending psychological isolation of a European commando in the bush often took its toll on the GCMA cadres. The commando feared only two scenarios: a mental or physical breakdown, or the possibility that one of his *maquisards* might be a secret member of the dreaded 421st Vietminh Intelligence Battalion, a special clandestine unit that gathered information on the GCMAs.

Despite the difficulties, Trinquier's GCMA commandos proved that the Vietminh, despite its organization and methods, did not command much popular support from Vietnam's diverse ethnic minorities. Highlanders devoted themselves to the French cause for two reasons: first, because the GCMA cadres allowed them to fight the imposition of an alien communist ideology; second, out of their hatred of the lowland Vietnamese, who had traditionally treated the highland *moi* (savages) with utter contempt. Vietnamese units hunting the GCMAs often burned whole native villages in reprisal for aiding the French-led commandos. GCMA units operating in the wake of the 1952 French debacle in the T'ai country found repeated reminders of Vietminh brutality – the heads of dead 6th Colonial paratroopers and T'ai partisans mounted on stakes along the French lines of retreat to the Black River.

From a few contact teams parachuted into the T'ai country in 1951, Trinquier's GCMA partisans grew to nearly 20,000 by late 1953, probably the largest single combat command led by any mere French Army major. In December 1953, the GCMA name was changed to Composite Intervention Groups (GMI, for *Groupement Mixte d'Intervention*) when the mission was extended beyond airborne commando operations. The GCMAs began to assume a strategic importance in the war, engaging in guerrilla actions over thousands of square miles of contested territory in Indochina. GCMA Meo guerrillas wrestled for control over Phong-Saly and Sam Neua provinces in Laos, two highland areas commanding the strategic upper Mekong River basin that had been uncontestable base areas for Vietminh-backed Pathet Lao.

and cut across Vietminh logistical lines. Farther west at Lai-Chau, GCMA units had established an airhead 200 miles behind Vietminh lines, controlling the shortest road from China to the gateway into Laos. Lai-Chau also served as an important re-supply base for Meo and T'ai GCMA units.

As GCMA units became widespread, thousands of native highlanders – Meo, Nung, Muong, T'ai, Hre and other little-known tribes – flocked to join Trinquier's *maquis* groups. Trinquier received far more native volunteers than his shoestring operation could absorb. With a few hundred tons of air-dropped supplies, his far-flung units consumed in a month what larger French garrisons consumed in a day, while tying down an equal or greater number of Vietminh main-force battalions.

In late 1953 Trinquier made ambitious plans to expand his GCMA strength to over 50,000 guerrillas within a year, hoping to exploit popular sentiment and retake the T'ai hill country during 1954-5. However, the French high command in Hanoi had a different use for the limited war supplies, plans that relegated the native irregulars and *maquis* groups to a relatively minor role. Before Trinquier could start his major GCMA expansion, necessary war matériel was being diverted to what Trinquier would call 'the regrettable Dienbienphu incident.'

Above: *A Vietminh supply column winds into a heavily forested communist enclave.*
Opposite top: *Major Bigeard (center) in the field with two of his subordinates.*
Below: *General Navarre and staff members on an inspection tour after Operation Castor.*

In October 1953, 600 Meo and T'ai GCMA commandos staged a dramatic raid on the important Vietminh supply center of Lao-Kay on the Sino-Vietnamese border, supported by a French paratroop drop and B-26 airstrikes. The commandos destroyed important war matériel and killed over 150 communists before melting back into the hills with the French paras. Vietminh troops took special care to avoid several GCMA *maquis* zones deep within their territory. The largest, the infamous Cardemon Zone, extended to the Chinese border

'Strike to Win'

Dienbienphu lay at the end of a long river valley astride the major invasion route into Laos. This remote outpost, hundreds of miles from the center of French military power inside the Red River Delta, had long served as an airhead into the Laotian interior. Some felt that Dienbienphu was well-situated to play this role for long-range GCMA Meo and T'ai partisans, and for French guerrilla operations into the mountain ridges straddling the Laos-Vietnam border.

In late 1953 the French commander-in-chief, General Henri Navarre, again sought an opportunity to snare Giap, with an eye toward improving the French negotiating position at a future settlement. Navarre ordered the investment of Dienbienphu to block an expected Vietminh invasion of Laos. His intention was to force Giap to hurl his main-force units into an elaborate 'kill zone.' But Navarre's ploy backfired, making Dienbienphu, in the words of Bernard Fall's famous account, 'hell in a very small place.'

In November 1953, a 4000-man French airborne assault, Operation CASTOR, easily recaptured Dienbienphu. After the French commander engaged in a highly publicized buildup, Giap took up the challenge, beginning a slow, methodical approach to Dienbienphu. Giap had assiduously avoided set-piece battles after his premature 1951 counteroffensive, but the Vietminh had since demonstrated increasing military sophistication. Logistically, larger formations could be sustained in the field for longer periods; a complex intelligence and communication apparatus, including a radio intercept unit, had been established; and with the help of experienced Communist Chinese advisors, anti-aircraft and artillery batteries were integrated into combat assault tactics. Giap felt confident in picking up the French challenge at Dienbienphu

that he could assemble on the battlefield resources superior to those of the French. His planning followed a strict and fundamental principle of revolutionary war borrowed from Mao: 'Strike to win, strike only when success is certain.'

Vietminh logistical preparation for battle required months of methodical road and depot construction through dense jungle hundreds of miles from major communist base areas. While Navarre poured thousands of paratroops, infantry, armor and artillery into Dienbienphu, GCMA commandos and mixed paratroop-partisan units engaged in long-range reconnaissance to track Vietminh progress toward the fortress.

These sorties, Operations REGATTA and POLLUX, were designed to probe and cut the long and vulnerable communist supply lines. To reconnoiter Giap's approach, scouts from Captain Tourret's elite 8th Parachute Assault Battalion sortied with local T'ai irregulars. This experiment benefited greatly from the natives' knowledge of the rugged terrain and local Vietminh activity, and provided Dienbienphu's commander, General de Castries, with timely, hard intelligence on Vietminh movements. By December 1953, French paras and irregulars skirmished outside Lai-Chau with the hard-core main-force troops of the 888th Battalion, 316th Vietminh Division. Linking up with local GCMA units, the recon teams began reporting a vise tightening around Dienbienphu.

The French high command seriously underestimated Vietminh offensive capabilities and preparations for battle. Within a month of Operation CASTOR, the 316th Vietminh Division and the 148th Vietminh Mountaineer Regiment (the communists also recruited among highlanders) struck the GCMA airhead at Lai-Chau before GCMA units mounted an assault on Vietminh lines of communi-

cation. Lai-Chau was abandoned in December 1953 by its sole defenders, 11 companies of T'ai irregulars. The Vietminh mountaineers dogged the 2100 retreating T'ai irregulars, hundreds of dependents and 36 French NCOs in a hellish 10-day fighting retreat toward Dienbienphu. Whole companies vanished without a trace in fierce but forgotten jungle skirmishes. Only 175 irregulars limped through Dienbienphu's gates to report that the ring had closed around the camp. The GCMA units committed to the battle fared little better. Although the 5000 long-range GCMA tied down Vietminh units three times their number, the French commandos failed to interdict lengthy communist supply lines that fed the Vietminh juggernaut closing on Dienbienphu. Although tactically effective and well-led in small-unit combat actions, the French-led guerrillas and partisans appeared too little, too late for any strategic impact on the climactic battle of the war.

Despite intense GCMA ground attack and French airstrikes, the entire Vietminh logistical system — from the Chinese railhead to the concentric circles burrowed around fortified French positions at Dienbienphu — proved impervious to interdiction. Thousands of impressed porters distributed supplies to assault units on bicycle and foot over crude roads hacked out of the jungle. The well-organized and -protected system delivered 100 tons per day to Giap's siege troops, a feat that sobered the French high command and foreshadowed a challenge to a succeeding generation of Western soldiers who would try to cut another logistical pipeline called the Ho Chi Minh Trail.

At Dienbienphu, the Vietminh demonstrated their complete mastery of unconventional warfare. Giap massed over 40,000 crack assault troops around the French fortifications to employ

Above: Communist troops launch a surprise attack against French machine gunners, who rush to position themselves for defense.
Opposite: A Vietnamese parachutist surveys the sky with a look of wonder, as French and Vietnamese comrades drop near Dienbienphu on 20 November 1953.

unorthodox military methods more akin to 17th-century siege tactics than to 20th-century revolutionary warfare. French preparations at the fortress were closely monitored by infiltrated agents wearing distinctive French camouflage battle dress. The ruse was so effective that communist agents knew in advance what color armbands the French forces wore on daily operations. Agents gleaned another astonishing piece of intelligence: French fortifications were constructed only of sandbags and wood, an indication that the French did not anticipate the presence of heavy Vietminh artillery.

Ingeniously, Vietminh artillery at Dienbienphu was employed not in Western-style massed interlocking fires, but by painstakingly dragging individual pieces into hillside escarpments. The hills overlooking the garrison soon bristled with heavy guns. Gunners took special care to leave foliage undisturbed so as to disguise the gun's location and its muzzle flash from both French counterfire and aerial reconnaissance. Tactical surprise was complete: in the battle's opening days, Vietminh artillery knocked out 40 percent of French artillery, destroyed 14 aircraft on Dienbienphu's airstrip and rendered the dirt runway useless. The French garrison's artillery commander, who had boasted of his gunners' prowess in taking on the Viets, soon afterward committed suicide by falling on a live grenade.

A desperate French airlift ensued after the Vietminh guns cratered the camp's airstrip. Instead of defending individual targets, communist anti-aircraft platoons trained their weapons offensively on a continuous 200-plane French airlift forced to fly into a murderous flak corridor to drop supplies on a shrinking garrison. Giap's AA platoons shot down 48 aircraft during the 56-day assault on Dienbienphu, including a C-119 flown by two American contract pilots. The pilots, flying for Civil Air Transport (CAT), a covert CIA airline, were the only American combat fatalities in the French-Vietminh war.

Flimsy French fortifications crumbled easily under the relentless pounding of communist artillery. One by one, the French strongholds gave way to Vietminh human-wave attacks. A dazzling array of zigzagging Vietminh siege trenches outflanked the garrison and choked it like a giant octopus. Following the dictum 'Isolate and overwhelm,' Giap's troops tightened the noose around Dienbienphu in March and April.

In mid-April General Navarre ordered Operation CONDOR, the relief of Dienbienphu. Inside the garrison, the 'paratroop Mafia' commanding the exhausted survivors planned a last-ditch breakout scheme. Operation CONDOR was originally planned as part of a relief operation to reinforce Dienbienphu's troops after they had smashed Giap's regiments. But the operation became a rescue mission instead. CONDOR consisted of four infantry battalions, reinforced by GCMA and GC commando units infiltrated into the Laotian jungle.

The mission of the GC and GCMA commandos under Lt Colonel Mollat was to pave the way for a rescue operation by screening for the regular battalions, and securing drop zones for a promised parachute drop by a Vietnamese airborne group. The 'Mollat Group' was divided into three units: an 800-man mixed GC made up of Lao and Meo under

Colonel Mollat, a 300-man GC led by a young Meo lieutenant named Vang Pao and 200 GCMAs under a French NCO. Also attached to CONDOR was an elite unit, the 610th Recon Commandos, on a special intelligence mission for the French high command. The same CAT C-119 aircraft contracted to fly over Dienbienphu also airdropped supplies to CONDOR.

By late April 1954, CONDOR had penetrated southwest of the Dienbienphu Valley to within 19 miles of the besieged fortress. However, promised airborne forces could not be committed; they were

Top: *Napalm bombs (first used in Indochina by the French) burst over trenches occupied by Vietminh attackers at Dienbienphu. French Union forces occupy the covered trenches in the foreground.*
Above: *One hundred pounds per man was the normal load for porters supplying Vietminh soldiers.*

Main picture: *The southern perimeter at Dienbienphu, where the French effort to seize and hold a forward base near Laos signaled the end of an Indochinese empire.*

Inset: *An unmarked Air America plane unloads wounded defenders of Dienbienphu at Luang Praban. Many of the wounded were not so fortunate as to be evacuated during the 56-day siege.*

Main picture: *A tank covers the advance of a French counterattack on Vietminh besiegers – 2 April 1954.*
Left: *As the 56-day siege wore on, it became increasingly difficult to evacuate the wounded and resupply the garrison due to shelling of the airstrip and effective use of anti-aircraft artillery. The Vietminh had transported these guns through the jungle against all odds.*
Right: *An underground communications post in the northwest sector of battered Dienbienphu, shortly before communist troops overran the fortress.*
Far right: *A column leaves Muong-Sair for Dienbienphu in an effort to create a diversion from the doomed French garrison: mid-April 1954.*

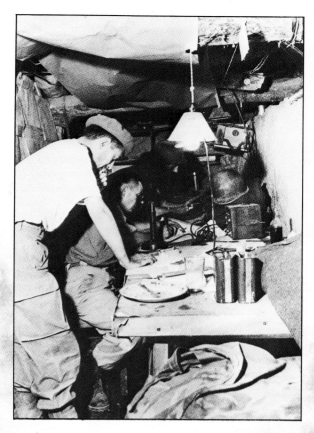

Main picture: *The Vietminh flag is planted in triumph on the French headquarters bunker at Dienbienphu in May of 1954.*
Above: *French Defense Minister Rene Pleven (left), Colonel Christian de Castries (center) and General Rene Cogny inspect positions at Dienbienphu in January 1954.*
Opposite top: *Captured French defenders leave Dienbienphu for prison camp.*

grounded by an acute shortage of transport aircraft in Hanoi. This shortage was due in part to a lone Vietminh sapper, who ingeniously infiltrated sewer tunnels beneath the large French airbase at Cat-Bi and blew up 18 badly needed aircraft. CONDOR never got off the ground.

On 7 May the Dienbienphu garrison was in its death throes. Endless waves of Vietminh infantry surged toward 'Isabelle,' the final French strongpoint held by 600 surviving Foreign Legionnaires of the crack 13th Demi-Brigade. Knowing the battle, indeed the war, was lost, the Legionnaires fixed bayonets for the last time and charged into Foreign Legion folklore.

Seventy-eight paras and Legionnaires managed to break out during the battle's last hours, or from the POW columns that were force-marched into communist POW camps. These stragglers, remnants of the elite 16,000-man French garrison, eventually linked up with roving GCMA guerrillas.

For many French troops, the fighting did not end with the signing of the cease-fire agreement in Geneva on 21 July 1954. After the armistice, a remorseful French high command broadcast painful orders to GCMA officers and NCOs: abandon the underground groups and fall back on Hanoi (the Geneva Accords prevented the French from re-supplying their long-range partisan units). Many French GCMA leaders ignored these orders. They fought on until the bitter end beside the native guerrillas – out of commitment, shared loyalty, or shame for their fellow Frenchmen who reluctantly abandoned the native *maquisards*. French irregulars resented what Major Tranquier called 'this bloodthirsty adventure.' In a bitter final operations report, Trinquier wrote that: 'Total suppression of logistical support will bring in its wake the progressive liquidation of our infiltrated elements. There is little hope of seeing the leaders of our *maquis* escape the "clemency" of Ho Chi Minh.'

Trinquier continued to believe his units should have continued the struggle. He chafed at 'ceasing operations as per orders...at the very moment they were about to triumph. Our *maquis*, undefeated on the battlefield, have been offered up in sacrifice.' American authorities reportedly turned down Trinquier's request that the United States (which never signed the Geneva Agreements) supply his guerrillas forces.

Some fortunate tribes, including the Nung or Muong, were able to fight their way to safety, owing to their relative proximity to major French military bases. Many of these tribesmen fled to the non-communist south to fight again under a different sponsor. But for the upland tribes – Meo, T'ai, Tho – the battle continued.

While French authorities disclaimed these remnants, communists were content to take counter-guerrilla operations into their own hands. They had committed some 15 main-force battalions, 15 regional battalions and 17 regional companies to the task by August 1954. Among these units hunting down the GCMA remnants was the dreaded 421st Vietminh Battalion. One by one, GCMA radio sets fell silent. In 1956 a chilling radio message, in perfect French, was picked up in South Vietnam: 'You sons-of-bitches, help us! Parachute us at least some ammunition so we can die like fighting men, not slaughtered like animals!'

Tragically, the last guerrillas of the First Indochina War were French-led irregulars.

Limbo War:
1954-60

The Geneva Accords, signed in July 1954, ended the French-Vietminh War, but launched a new round of intrigues in Indochina. By internationalizing the colonial conflict, the five-power Geneva Conference became a focus for a larger East-West geopolitical struggle. By involving American, Soviet and Chinese strategic interests, the Conference sowed the seeds of a second major Indochina war.

Ho Chi Minh left the conference table at Geneva with much less than his Vietminh had won in battle. Although his forces controlled much of the countryside in both north and south, he reluctantly settled for a Vietnam divided at the 17th parallel – very close to the old lines drawn at Potsdam in 1945. Geneva clearly eclipsed Ho's dream for a unified Vietnam under communist rule.

Covert 'Stay Behind' Networks

Ho's chief sponsor at Geneva was the Soviet Union. But Moscow had its own political agenda that included seeking French aid in scuttling the US-backed proposal for a European Defense Community (EDC). By vetoing the EDC, France gained quiet Soviet support for a Vietnam divided into a communist North and a Western-backed regime in the South. This arrangement allowed France both to save face and to maintain a strong political influence in Indochina. Another result of Geneva was the installation of ostensibly neutral non-communist governments in South Vietnam, Laos and Cambodia. The United States, now rapidly replacing France as the dominant Western influence in Southeast Asia, supported these shaky non-communist regimes as a way to halt further Communist gains in the region.

The Geneva Accords changed all the rules governing conduct of the war. Before July 1954, both the French and Vietminh had treated Indochina as a single geographic unit, irrespective of national borders. But the International Control Commission (ICC) – set up to supervise foreign advisory missions and police military activities across borders – soon forced both communist and Western-backed regimes to expand their covert unconventional warfare capabilities to secure clandestinely those political objectives not won at Geneva.

Even the most passive Geneva requirement – the 300-day population 'regroupment period' – became a vehicle for East-West intrigue. Nearly 900,000 Vietnamese, mostly anti-communist Catholics, elected to resettle in the South, while 90,000 Vietminh 'regroupees' left behind families to march

Previous pages: Years of intrigue and 'palace revolutions' in Saigon – this one in 1962 – destabilized the South Vietnamese Government and contributed to the communist victory.
Top: North Vietnamese welcome their army to Haiphong in May 1955.
Above: Three months later, victorious North Vietnamese soldiers enter Hong-Gay.

north and eventually be absorbed into the 324th and 325th North Vietnamese Army (NVA) Divisions. Mindful of the political weakness and confusion in the South, Ho Chi Minh ordered underground some 10,000 Southern communist agents, who also buried for future use enough weapons in hidden caches to field about 6000 guerrillas in the South. These 'former resistance cadres' set about destablizing the fledging South Vietnamese nation, initially through overt political agitation and propaganda, then, as necessary, via covert underground political action – which included such traditional Vietminh weapons as armed propaganda, assassination and terrorism. Clandestine 'stay-behind' networks provided the seeds of an 'indigenous' Southern insurgency if Ho decided to activate one, and served as his insurance policy against the failure of the 1956 elections designed by the Geneva Accords to unify Vietnam peacefully. Had these elections been held in 1954, the result would have been an easy victory for the Vietminh.

Even American officials had concluded that South Vietnam should probably 'be written off as a loss.' Western intelligence services recognized that Ho

was a good bet to win the 1956 elections unless the United States could cement a viable anti-communist Southern alternative to Ho's brand of communism. A US Military Advisory Assistance Group (MAAG), established to begin training a viable South Vietnamese Army on a crash basis, was limited by the Geneva Accords to a 342-man ceiling. MAAG was augmented by an ICC-approved Temporary Equipment Recovery Mission (TERM) which increased the ICC ceiling by 300 personnel. Formed to straighten out the logistical mess created by the French withdrawal, TERM also served as a useful vehicle to skirt the Geneva limits of foreign military advisors and US intelligence operatives.

CIA Involvement Deepens

The cutting edge of the US effort to fashion a workable South Vietnamese Government was the Saigon Military Mission (SMM), led by Air Force Colonel Edward G Lansdale. Ostensibly the US Embassy's assistant air attaché, Lansdale was actually an innovative CIA intelligence officer with a growing reputation as a creative field operative. A former

A harmless-looking well is plumbed for evidence of a booby-trapped tunnel, which could be as much as 20 feet down, below water level.

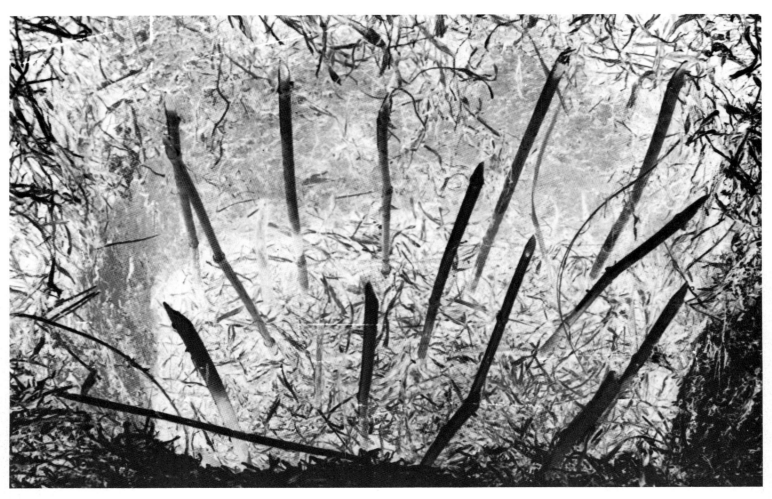

*An ancient and lethal trap
of a type widely used in
Vietnam – the sharpened
bamboo stakes are
implanted in the bottom of a
pit and concealed by
camouflage.
Opposite: American
involvement in Vietnam
brought sophisticated
weapons and technology,
and training in how to use
them, to South Vietnamese
popular forces.*

advertising man, Lansdale served as an OSS officer in World War II and elected to stay in the service thereafter. He joined the newly created Air Force in 1947 because he felt that 'There would be more elbow room for fresh ideas in the air force than in the older services.'

As an advisor to the Philippine government in the early 1950s, Lansdale played a key role in defeating a communist rebellion by Huk insurgents and promoting the emergence of the charismatic Ramon Magsaysay as Philippine president. During the anti-Huk campaign, Lansdale instructed Filipino army troops in unconventional warfare methods and developed sophisticated psywar techniques into a virtual art form. In one Huk-controlled area, Lansdale played upon local superstitions by circulating vampire stories. Filipino troops then strung up a dead Huk guerrilla, draining blood from two puncture wounds in the neck and leaving the corpse for the Huks to find; the insurgents cleared out of the area. Lansdale's colorful exploits inspired two best-selling Cold War novels, *The Ugly American* and the more cynical *The Quiet American*.

Lansdale's 'Cold War Combat Team' arrived in Saigon quietly soon after the fall of Dienbienphu. The original SMM mission – to assist the Vietnamese in paramilitary and psywar operations against the Vietminh – was rapidly overtaken by the events at Geneva. The new mission focused on preparing covert paramilitary teams for action in communist-controlled Tonkin, soon to be evacuated by the French.

The CIA saw great potential in SMM sponsorship of Vietnamese unconventional warfare units. Despite several previous US initiatives, uneasy Franco-American relations – largely due to mutual suspicions by French and American intelligence services – had barred American entry into this field. The *Deuxieme Bureau*'s vivid recollection of the OSS in World War II had soured its relationship with the successor organization, the CIA. French distrust was such that General de Lattre, in a 1951 visit to Washington, secured agreement that prohibited CIA operations in Indochina without explicit French consent.

The French also resisted US suggestions for a role in training unconventional units because 'The natives resented French colonialism.' Even US Army brass received the idea with little enthusiasm, believing that American-trained irregulars could not crack the firm communist police organization in Vietminh-controlled areas. When in 1951 the CIA suggested to de Lattre that he form 'counter-guerrilla' groups to operate inside Vietminh territory, the French general demurred, although similar principles were soon applied to GCMA *maquis* units. The GCMA legacy (even as these units, in 1954, were struggling against Vietminh efforts to exterminate them) proved that irregular clandestine units could be employed by both sides for deep penetration of enemy territory. With the fielding of the SMM, the CIA prepared to fill the vacuum created by the departing French. Bitter Vietnamese anti-communists turned to the SMM for help in establishing a resistance movement in Tonkin.

Opposite: *The Mekong Delta was a battleground in every phase of the Vietnam War. Its numberless waterways and heavy vegetation offered concealment to communist guerrillas and their pursuers, including the US Navy SEALs seen here on a search-and-destroy mission.*

Below: *Psychological warfare characterized the struggle for Vietnam. Here, a MAAG psywar advisor and his Vietnamese assistant load propaganda leaflets into the dispersal chute of a C-47 aircraft during a spying mission.*

SMM was on a tight schedule. Within a month of the Geneva conference, Vietminh operatives had started secretly taking control of Hanoi and other Tonkinese areas still held by French military forces. Before the 300-day Geneva regroupment period ended, the 10-man SMM located, selected and ex-filtrated two paramilitary teams, code-named Binh and Hao. Both teams trained at CIA bases in the Pacific, including one in the Philippine Islands set up by 'Freedom Company,' a non-profit Filipino organization backed by Lansdale's old friend, President Magsaysay. Freedom Company also supplied SMM with Filipinos experienced in anti-guerrilla fighting. Binh and Hao training consisted of trademark CIA instructions in sabotage, quick-kill techniques, explosives and undercover survival.

Most of Lansdale's team had experience in para-military and clandestine intelligence operations, although none could match Lansdale's flare for political-psychological warfare. Lansdale assigned Major Lucien Conein to the important task of developing the Binh organization in the North. Conein was the same American guerrilla fighter who had led Project COMORE's French-Vietnamese commandos against Japanese military installations in 1945. He had previously served as a Foreign Legionnaire before joining the US Army in 1940. Volunteering for OSS duty, Conein received expert training by Britain's Special Operations Executive (SOE) for behind-the-lines missions in World War II. As part of Lansdale's SMM, Conein and his team were assigned to MAAG's Hanoi branch for cover purposes. Their overt mission was to direct a refugee airlift; their covert mission was to organize Binh as an underground guerrilla force for assigned

missions after French withdrawal. Major Fred Allen directed the Hao group, whose mission was to organize anti-Vietminh resistance farther south for later penetration into North Vietnam, and additionally, to keep in contact with other Vietnamese revolutionary groups in the South.

The Geneva regroupment period provided the perfect cover for SMM preparations, including the infiltration and supply of paramilitary teams. Civil Air Transport (CAT), the CIA-owned airline, had secured, with Lansdale's help, a French contract to airlift Catholic refugees from Tonkin to the South. While the refugee-ferrying business kept CAT pilots constantly in the air, they could provide covert transport for Lansdale's Binh and Hao groups. As refugees went from North to South, returning CAT aircraft carried weapons, special equipment and explosives needed to execute SMM missions. Conein's team handled CAT arms shipments at the Hanoi end.

It was not the first time CAT had flown double duty, transporting refugees and running guns, nor would it be the last. CAT, later known as Air America or simply AA, had its roots in Major General Claire Chennault's World-War-II American Volunteer Group (AVG) – the famous Flying Tigers – which harassed Japanese planes against overwhelming odds in China. General Chennault's AVG could be called the world's first 'aerial guerrilla force.' Chennault started CAT in 1947 with a batch of US-surplus C-47 Douglas Dakota and C-46 Curtis Commando transport planes, manned by veteran World War II pilots with a thirst for adventure. CAT flew guns, ammunition and relief supplies for Chiang Kai-shek's Chinese Nationalist forces in

President Ngo Dinh Diem (flanked by US Ambassador Nolting and Commander Ivar A Johnson in this 1962 photo) had strong American backing when he took power in 1954. His reputation as a Vietnamese nationalist was so high that Ho Chi Minh had once asked Diem to join his government.

Before the final French withdrawal from Hanoi, Conein's Binh team infiltrated Tonkin by CAT aircraft and US Navy Task Force 98, which also smuggled caches of arms and high explosives up Tonkin's rivers and coastlines. The combined forces delivered over 8 tons of clandestine supplies to Binh, including 14 radios, 300 carbines, 50 pistols, 100,000 rounds of ammunition and over 300 pounds of high explosives.

Under Conein's direction, Binh established its base and prepared for the 'delayed sabotage' of North Vietnam's transportation network – bus lines and railroad system – by contaminating engine oil and undermining maintenance facilities and equipment. Binh received some assistance in this task from special CIA technicians flown in from Hawaii. The group also took extensive notes of potential targets for future paramilitary activities, since American adherence to the letter of the Geneva Accords precluded 'active' sabotage against Tonkin's power plants, water facilities, harbors and bridges. Meanwhile, Vietminh sappers were busily engaged in their own active sabotage against similar facilities in the South.

However, the operational life of the undercover Binh and Hao agents who penetrated the North was short. Due to the strictly regimented communist society (that extended even down to the smallest village), Vietminh counterintelligence units rolled up these teams within a few years. Subsequent CIA efforts to insert Vietnamese agents into North Vietnam achieved limited short-term success, but eventually met with the same fate.

Lansdale's team also engineered 'black' psywar operations directed against departing Vietminh regroupees and in soon-to-be-communist-controlled territory. One successful 'psywar strike' in Hanoi involved distributing purported Vietminh leaflets with instructions on proper civilian behavior and on property and monetary reforms that would follow the Vietminh assumption of power. Within days the fake leaflet had tripled refugee registration and drastically devalued Vietminh currency. The SMM leaflets were so authentic-looking – even to Vietminh rank and file – that the populace dismissed subsequent denunciations of the leaflet by Vietminh Radio as a French propaganda trick. Another psywar strike employed noted Vietnamese astrologers hired to predict disastrous futures for Vietminh leaders and programs while foreseeing success for those supporting Southern unity.

The SMM also formed the Vietnamese National Army's 1st Armed Propaganda Company to conduct its own black psywar strikes in Vietminh territory. Dressed as peasants, the propaganda company infiltrated southern Vietminh zones to distribute leaflets attributed to the Vietminh Resistance Committee, reassuring Vietminh embarking on Polish and Russian ships for the north that they would be kept safe below decks from imperialist air and submarine attacks and asking troops to bring warm clothing. A follow-up rumor campaign linked the warm-clothing request to the disinformation that Vietminh were being shipped to Manchuria as railroad workers. Intelligence reports later confirmed that local Vietminh committees had sharply protested the 'deportation to the north.'

Each of these ploys bore the indelible imprint of

their war against Mao's communists, and ended up transporting thousands of refugees as Chiang's armies collapsed. CAT pilots had to be both rugged and brave, servicing their own planes and flying off dirt airstrips and abandoned World War II runways. Piloting a CAT 'rice-run' was no milk run, but a dangerous business, as Chinese Communists frequently peppered unarmed CAT aircraft delivering food and medical supplies as well as ammo to Chiang's troops.

In backing the losing side in the Chinese Civil War, CAT faced bankruptcy in 1950 when the CIA stepped in to become its new owner. Agency personnel had often flown as passengers in CAT planes to far-flung battlefields in China. The CIA viewed the airline as a perfect cover and a potential money-maker as well. CAT was reorganized as a Delaware corporation, administered from offices in Washington DC, and headquartered in Taipei, Taiwan, where the CIA proprietary found shelter with the sympathetic government-in-exile of Chiang Kai-shek. CAT functioned as a legitimate airline, flying regular routes throughout Asia, including Tokyo, Bangkok and Hong Kong. It prospered during the Korean War boom and by 1954 was the most profitable airline in the Far East. But CAT's profit-making operations masked its real function as the CIA's private aerial paramilitary force. Its demonstrated capability suited the CIA's ever-expanding role in backing worldwide paramilitary ventures. CAT airlifted over 15,000 French troops into Dienbienphu in late 1953 and later flew leased US C-119 'Flying Boxcars' through the gauntlet of Vietminh anti-aircraft guns to resupply the doomed garrison. The CIA had acquired CAT with the understanding that it would divest itself of the airline as soon as it was feasible. But the CIA's involvement in Southeast Asia over the next quarter-century guaranteed that Civil Air Transport, aka Air America (and its worldwide subsidiaries, Intermountain Air and Southern Air Transport), found plenty to keep it busy.

Colonel Lansdale. Black psywar strikes targeted the uneducated masses – whose support was crucial to the success of both communist and non-communist regimes. The communists perfected their own form of delayed sabotage. Ho Chi Minh's Central Committee of the Lao Dong (Communist) Party placed a high priority on subverting the fledging South Vietnamese Army, perhaps the only vehicle in the South with the organization and communications to forge a viable nation. In a secret struggle to subvert the National Army, the Central Committee dispatched 100 specially trained communist cadres to infiltrate army ranks and wreck Army-Peasant relations. Only years later would these 'moles' – in some cases high-ranking South Vietnamese officers involved in key pacification projects – be unmasked. Such actions encouraged later suspicion and paranoia among South Vietnamese elites.

A few years after Lansdale's SMM, far more sophisticated (but no more effective) techniques would struggle to 'win the hearts and minds' of Vietnamese peasants in a sharp contest with Ho's underground 'resistance cadres.'

When Lansdale's SMM arrived in Saigon, the South Vietnamese nation existed only on paper; it was more accurately a checkerboard of independent political fiefdoms held together by self-interest and French military subsidies. Ngo Dinh Diem, American-backed leader for South Vietnam, assumed power in July 1954 with the blessing of American political leaders and few others. Most seasoned foreign observers gave odds that Diem, an insecure monkish Catholic, would be a temporary leader of a short-lived nation.

The unassuming man who undertook the awesome task of pulling a South Vietnamese nation together was a Vietnamese nationalist of such stature that Ho Chi Minh had once asked him to join his government (Diem refused). He was chosen for the post of prime minister in the new South Vietnamese regime over the objections of the French, who knew Diem as fiercely anti-French. The Catholic Diem, although not exactly pro-American, was the US choice; during a trip to the United States in the early 1950s, he had courted (and been courted by) influential Americans including President Dwight D Eisenhower, Senator Mike Mansfield, and a young Massachusetts senator named John F Kennedy.

Diem's selection as prime minister did not leave the French without influence in Saigon. They still held a strong hand through their military support of the sect armies as paid *suppletifs* and of national Army Chief of Staff, General Nguyen Van Hinh. A Francophile, General Hinh held French citizenship, had a French wife and had served honorably in the French Air Force. He was loudly plotting Diem's ouster in autumn 1954, encouraged by elements of the *Deuxieme Bureau* openly hostile to the anti-French Vietnamese prime minister.

The Diem-Hinh power struggle took on the added flavor of a barely concealed competition between the *Deuxieme Bureau* and the CIA. The cloak-and-dagger struggle in Saigon pitted French-backed surrogates – General Hinh, the sect armies and portions of the national army – against Diem and Catholic militia, supported by the SMM. An added wild card was the role of southern communists, who

Top: *Here, a captured communist assassin, masked to prevent recognition, leads allied soldiers to the hiding place of fellow guerrillas.*

Above: *A South Vietnamese villager, wounded in a cross-fire between government and communist forces, is brought in for treatment by his wife. Because the*

Vietnam conflict combined the worst aspects of both civil and guerrilla warfare, daily life for the common people – never easy – became an even greater struggle.

had established secret liaison with the sects to encourage armed force against Diem – while avoiding direct opposition themselves. It was a low-risk, high-payoff strategy, the objective of which was to destabilize the Diem regime without actively violating the Geneva Agreements or exposing covert cadre structures that might be needed as a nucleus for a future armed struggle.

Lansdale knew both Diem and Hinh personally and attempted to set up a reconciliation, while SMM officers maintained contacts with Hinh's chief deputies. The two most important pro-Hinh officers were Lt Colonel Lan, a French agent who was suspected of employing his special-force commandos as 'action squads' dispensing terrorism against political opponents, and Captain Giai, head of the National Army G-5 (Psywar), who was suspected of using army leaflet and broadcast facilities to dispense anti-Diem propaganda. After reconciliation talks between Diem and Hinh failed, Hinh set a date for Diem's overthrow: 26 October 1954. SMM agents detected Hinh's preparations and whisked Lt Colonel Lan and Captain Giai off to the Philippines on the pretext of an official visit to study Filipino anti-guerrilla operations. With Hinh's key agents abroad, 26 October passed without an attack on Diem's palace. Under strong American pressure, General Hinh and his fellow conspirators soon departed for exile in France.

In January 1955, after prolonged negotiations, a combined US-French training mission, known as the Training Relations & Instruction Mission (TRIM), was established to smooth over Franco-American rivalries and get on with the task of training a modern South Vietnamese Army. With a growing emphasis on pacification, US Ambassador J Lawton 'Lightning Joe' Collins and MAAG Chief Lt General 'Iron Mike' O'Daniel transferred Lansdale from the Embassy staff to head up TRIM's key National Security Action division, charged with co-ordinating all US civilian and military efforts in Vietnam.

To Lansdale, national security began with Prime Minister Ngo Dinh Diem. SMM knew the long-term threat came from clandestine Vietminh agents honeycombing the South with organized cells – the initial step toward a new people's war. But in early 1955, SMM agents discovered that the sects had formed a 'United Sect Front' to move against the South Vietnamese leader. The odds were heavily stacked against Diem pulling together the chaotic South Vietnamese body politic. Even Ambassador Collins believed the US should dump Diem.

Saigon itself was a faction-riddled city, with numerous private armies jealously guarding entire regions around the capital. Armed to the teeth by the French, these groups, encouraged by colonialist elements in the French military and the *Deuxieme Bureau*, stood in line to oust Diem.

The sect armies jockeying for power traced roots back to the Japanese occupation, when they were secretly trained and armed (against the French) by the *Kempeitai*, the Japanese Army's secret police. Uneasy alliances formed with the Vietminh in 1946 quickly dissolved after a combination of communist strongarm tactics and political opportunism brought these nominally anti-French groups over to the French.

The most notoriously opportunistic were the Binh Xuyen, a mafia of river pirates led by kingpin Bay Vien, whom Lansdale later characterized as 'a combination of Boss Tweed and Al Capone.' Binh Xuyen gangsters controlled the Saigon River approaches, as well as the city's lucrative gambling and prostitution parlors, with a 6000-man army divided into 15 400-man battalions. Bay Vien's influence was far-reaching; he managed to buy control of the Saigon police force from the absentee playboy emperor Bao Dai (who rode out the 1955 crisis living in luxury on the French Riviera), and was a brigadier general in the national army. Bay Vien also had powerful friends inside the French security services, who provided the Binh Xuyen with a generous supply of automatic weapons, 60mm mortars and three French *vedette* gunboats.

The Hoa Hao and Cao Dai were quasi-religious sects, each of which controlled large tracts of territory in the South. The Hoa Hao, a rowdy sect of dissident Buddhists, had broken with the Vietminh after the communists assassinated its spiritual leader in 1947 for refusing to submit to communist political control. During the war against the Vietminh, the French armed some 20,000 Hoa Hao troops, who were led by a colorful rebel general, 'Ba Cut' (for 'cut finger' – the finger joint he hacked off to demonstrate his commitment to Vietnamese independence). General Hinh, in his struggle against Diem, had made Ba Cut a National Army colonel, while Bay Vien had given the Hoa Hao rebel operational control over his own green-bereted Binh Xuyen battalions. The Cao Dai was another quasi-religious sect whose patron saints included Jesus Christ, the Buddha, Confucius, Sun Yat-sen and Victor Hugo. The Cao Dai's 15,000-man army, secretly trained and armed by the Japanese during the war, controlled vast territories in the rubber-tree forests north of Saigon as a virtual state within a state.

Lansdale, as he had done with Magsaysay, developed a close relationship with Diem, aiding him in his search for reliable units in the anticipated sect struggle. Since the army's loyalty was questionable, Diem installed reliable Tonkinese militia, mostly Catholic refugees from the north, near his Doc Lap palace. But these units were clearly no match for the sects. To supplement the militia, Lansdale arranged with Magsaysay for Filipino assistance in training Diem's Presidential Guard Battalion.

Lansdale, his 'Boy Scout' image notwithstanding, had plunged deeply into internecine Saigon politics, and his aid to Diem had stepped on many toes. The Saigon rumor mill pegged the American as the source of virtually every political intrigue afoot in the capital. Lansdale, perhaps a victim of his own reputation and success at black psywar strikes, was amused by some of the wilder tales, many spread by his nemeses in the French intelligence services. Lansdale also received dire warnings of hidden assassins stalking him. In Saigon's highly charged, deadly environment, warnings of kidnappings and murders usually had some validity. More than once Lansdale was 'invited' by thugs to meet with Bay Vien or other anti-Diem leaders. Assassins did trail the American cold warrior, who usually kept a small .25-caliber pistol or a hand grenade within reach. One unfortunate Frenchman resembling Lansdale

Top: *A Vietnamese Air Force B-26 bomber armed with two napalm bombs, two rocket pods and eight .50-caliber machine guns.*
Left: *South Vietnamese laborers fill sandbags at My Phuc Tay.*

Above: *A Republic of Vietnam Civil Defense Group trainee takes part in an ambush exercise. Such military-civilian efforts under US auspices (1955 onward) were first headed up by TRIM (Training Relations & Instruction Mission).*

was machine-gunned at point-blank range on a Saigon street; on another occasion, Lansdale heard a whizzing bullet pass inches from his head.

Lansdale's SMM also worked hard to convince sect commanders to bring their troops over to the government. By resorting to nationalist appeals, anti-French sentiment, or just plain bribes, Lansdale's operatives convinced almost half the 40,000 anti-Diem troops around Saigon to integrate into the National Army by March 1955. This, too, was a dangerous business; one Binh Xuyen colonel who committed his four battalions to Diem was savagely beaten with chains, kidnapped and never seen again.

Lansdale personally delivered to Diem's side a dissident force of Cao Dai, known as the Lien Minh, who fought against both the Vietminh and the French. The Lien Minh's commander, Trinh Minh The, initiated contact in 1954 with Lansdale, who traveled secretly to the guerrillas' hideout to negotiate for CIA funding of The's 3000-man operation. Trinh Minh The followed up Lansdale's visit with one of his own, escaping a determined French police dragnet in the process. Lansdale, impressed by the gutsy guerrilla leader, persuaded The and another Cao Dai commander with 8000 armed troops to integrate their units into Diem's army.

Tension in Saigon came to a head in March 1955, after Bay Vien and the sect front decided to replace Diem and divide power among themselves. Bay Vien issued an ultimatum to Diem. Binh Xuyen mortar rounds fell on Doc Lap Palace, and army troops took up positions in the streets facing Binh Xuyen soldiers. A hastily arranged cease-fire by French and American authorities lasted several ten-

sion-filled weeks. In the interim, while Bay Vien's political maneuvering against Diem continued, Lien Minh agents in black pajamas penetrated Binh Xuyen strongholds to collect intelligence.

In April 1955, with full support of the army, Diem moved against the sects. After a series of street battles that lasted into May, Diem's forces routed the Binh Xuyen forces and broke the back of the independent sect armies. The National Army drove the disorganized remnants, some 2500 Binh Xuyen, Cao Dai and Hoa Hao, into the Rung Ro swamps and other former Vietminh base areas, where they became minor paramilitary auxiliaries under communist control. Sect remnants, according to communist sources, soon dwindled into a token force deemed politically unreliable and 'decadent' by Vietnamese communists.

By mid-1955 Diem, to the surprise of most Western observers, appeared to be consolidating his power. Yet the often-heralded 'miracle of Diem' would probably not have been possible without the help of Lansdale's SMM. Diem felt secure enough in building a separate South Vietnamese nation to refuse – with US encouragement – to hold the Geneva-sponsored elections in 1956. Diem, who had stated that democratic elections could not be held in communist North Vietnam, held his own election and became President of the Republic of Vietnam.

Diem and his American advisors anticipated that Ho Chi Minh would attempt eventually to unify Vietnam by force under communist rule. The crushing of the independent sect armies and the final departure of French troops in April 1956 allowed the US MAAG to develop an effective Army of the Republic of Vietnam (ARVN) along conventional US Army lines. The new army consisted of six divisions – three full-sized and three 'light' territorial divisions – backed by a part-time paramilitary militia (the Self-Defense Corps) and full-time regional police units (the Civil Guard).

The new ARVN also contained a special unconventional warfare unit, the 1st Observation Group, established in February 1956. Based on the old Binh concept, 1st Observation Group was a 300-man special-forces unit trained by the CIA to operate

Left: *President Diem broadcasts an announcement that the divisive sect armies of South Vietnam must yield to a single national army (March 1955). Days later, sect forces did merge – for an abortive coup against the government.*

Top right: *South Vietnamese forces in the Rung Sat await President Diem's review early in his regime.*
Right: *An ARVN soldier destroys captured Vietcong propaganda during a raid in the Camau Peninsula.*

undercover in small 15-man teams. In the event of a conventional North Vietnamese invasion across the DMZ (the Demilitarized Zone on the 17th parallel), teams were prepared to act as 'stay-behind' units and recruit GCMA-type insurgents for harassment of North Vietnamese Army (NVA) units. As a highly specialized elite force, 1st Observation Group enjoyed a privileged status, reporting not through regular ARVN channels but directly to President Ngo Dinh Diem himself via secret radio hookups.

Even as the CIA trained 1st Observation Group, US military intelligence officers had concluded that the likeliest threat from North Vietnam would come from a resumption of a clandestine people's war in South Vietnam, rather than a conventional Korean-type invasion over the heavily defended DMZ. In such a covert war, 'stay-behind' cadres would be activated, supported by infiltration from the North.

Diem launched a 'Communist Denunciation Campaign' in 1956, targeting 10,000 underground cadres for elimination. Once again, SMM-sponsored organizations like Freedom Company, 'Operation Brotherhood,' and the Eastern Construction Company assisted Diem. Operation Brotherhood was an organization of Free World volunteer medical teams; the Eastern Construction Company, a Freedom Company spinoff, provided 500 hard-core Filipino anti-communist technicians to help rebuild the war-torn South. SMM quietly monitored these so-called civic action operations. Although designed to improve roads, medical care, food distribution and government assistance, these groups performed a secondary role by engaging in subtle psywar, and aided Diem's army and police forces in targeting and eliminating Vietminh stay-behind cadres, while demonstrating the government's concern for the peasantry.

Diem's aggressive Denunciation Campaign and harsh Law 10/59 (which outlawed most forms of revolutionary opposition), plus the civic action groups, helped whittle away at underground cadres, now derisively called 'Vietcong,' a pejorative term for Vietnamese Communist. By 1959 Communist Party membership in the South had dwindled to about 5000, with only some 2000 men under arms, mostly veteran Vietminh, 'decadent' sect remnants and dissident highlanders.

Faced with imminent destruction, southern cadres were ordered by Hanoi to start armed propaganda and recruitment among peasants. Aided by infiltration of several hundred northern party cadres, the Vietcong then unleashed a terror-and-assassination campaign against government officials, teachers and village chiefs. Over 2500 assassinations took place in 1959, more than double the previous year. Sabotage and terror, previously localized, became widespread.

In May 1959, the Lao Dong Central Committee in Hanoi formally authorized an 'armed struggle' in the South. A secret, composite engineer unit, the 559th Transportation & Support Group (known as *Doan* 559) was dispatched to prepare for large-scale infiltration through Laos and by sea. From 1959 to 1964, an estimated 44,000 regroupees – Vietminh who had gone North in 1954 – skirted the heavily defended DMZ and slipped into Vietnam by way of Laos on what would soon become famous in the West as the Ho Chi Minh Trail.

Covert War in Laos

During the late 1950s, North Vietnam took advantage of a deteriorating political situation in neighboring Laos among rightists, neutralists and communists to seize the strategic Laotian panhandle regions that could support large-scale infiltration into South Vietnam. After the 1954 Geneva Conference, an estimated 7000 Vietminh troops remained inside Laos illegally, as the backbone of the communist Pathet Lao guerrilla movement. North Vietnamese/Pathet Lao forces were able to wrest control over the mountain town of Tchepone from the inept Royal Lao Army in 1957. From Vietminh experience in Laos, the communists knew that Tchepone was the key crossroads of a trail network leading into South Vietnam's Central Highlands and the Mekong Delta 'rice bowls.' The narrow, rugged mountain trails safely skirted the easily monitored DMZ, and appeared to be relatively secure from interdiction. More importantly, Tchepone gave the North Vietnamese control over the strategic heartland of Southeast Asia, and the ability to regulate the flow of infiltration over a long, undefended South Vietnamese border.

Prevented by the Geneva Agreements from maintaining a large military advisory mission in Laos, the United States had established a Program Evaluation Office (PEO) in 1958 as the chief instrument of US clandestine political and military involvement. The PEO was a CIA cover for a wide range of covert actions against the Pathet Lao and its North Vietnamese sponsors. PEO was the embodiment of the CIA philosophy that the only way to combat communism in places like Laos was through covert political action and paramilitary groups – in the Lansdale tradition. Part of the PEO mission included cultivation of the highlanders straddling the Lao-North Vietnamese border – the same tribes organized and later abandoned by the French.

In order to bring ethnic representation to a CIA-backed Lao political organization, PEO operatives sought out the Meo tribesmen – the largest single tribal group in Laos that made its living from cultivating opium poppies. Meo chief Vang Pao, who had commanded a French *Groupement Commando* near Dienbienphu in 1954, at first remained skeptical of the CIA offer of direct support to undertake guerrilla operations against communist supply lines. He recalled the harsh treatment the Meo had suffered from the communists for previous involvement with the French, but most of all, how the French abandoned and disarmed the Meo after Dienbienphu. To a proud Meo warrior, weapons meant honor and prestige; Vang Pao's men still carried ancient flintlock rifles. The chieftain asked for CIA assurances that his people would not be abandoned once support began. Perhaps naively, the CIA officers promised Vang Pao continued support and pledged not to confiscate any weapons provided.

As a token gesture, the PEO representatives asked Vang Pao about his immediate needs; the tribal chief requested a large anvil (so the Meo could forge farm tools) and blankets for his people. Soon Air America planes dropped the requested anvil and 50,000 military-surplus wool sweaters to the Meo. On a subsequent flight, AA pilots were surprised to

discover a sea of olive-drab tribesmen waving furiously at their new benefactors.

By 1959 PEO had developed a small pilot program for Meo guerrillas and began intelligence-gathering operations in scattered mountain villages near the strategic Plain of Jars. In July 1959, 107 US Special Forces, under the command of Lt Colonel Arthur 'Bull' Simons, arrived in Laos to train 12 Royal Lao Army battalions and Lao paramilitary groups in behind-the-lines warfare. Attempts to disguise these Special Forces WHITE STAR teams under PEO cover did not fool the North Vietnamese. Upon their arrival, Radio Hanoi broadcast that

The rich Mekong River Delta was the target of communist infiltration through Laos by way of Tchepone.

'The United States has invaded Laos.' Thus the 'secret war' in Laos began.

With a handful of CIA case officers, and the aid of an elite 99-man Thai Border Police unit, the WHITE STAR teams organized over 9000 Meo in the first year. Soon Meo guerrillas were blowing up communist supply dumps and harassing NVA/ Pathet Lao logistics lines. Even in Sam Neua province, a long-time Pathet Lao stronghold, Meo guerrillas established Site 118 atop a steep mountain at Phou Pha Thi. Supplied by Air America helicopters and planes, the Phou Pha Thi garrison held out against repeated Pathet Lao assaults until 1975.

The small pilot Meo program soon grew into the largest clandestine army in CIA history. Within ten years, the Meo army under Vang Pao expanded to over 40,000 guerrillas and became the most effective irregular fighting force in Laos. To support the Meo and other tribal guerrillas, like the T'ai and Kha tribes, CIA's Air America increased its clandestine services, flying covert missions over China, North Vietnam and, increasingly, as the Ho Chi Minh Trail expanded, over the Laotian panhandle. When the Trail doubled its capacity in 1961, the 'limbo war' of the 1950s had entered a newer, more deadly phase.

Advisory War: 1960-64

Edward Lansdale, now a brigadier general (USAF) and Pentagon assistant for special operations, revisited Vietnam in early January of 1961 to assess the situation. While his concern for Vietnam was genuine, personally, he also welcomed the occasion to avoid any association with the pending Bay of Pigs fiasco. What he found alarmed him; he reported that during 1960 the Vietcong had infiltrated thousands of armed forces into South Vietnam, recruited local levies of military terroritorials and guerrillas and undertaken large-scale guerrilla and terroristic operations. The number of South Vietnamese government officials assassinated had risen by several thousand over the preceding year, and President Diem, apparently unable to do anything but antagonize his non-communist opposition, had barely survived an 11 November 1960 coup staged by officers of his elite airborne brigade. The trend was 'downhill and dangerous,' threatening anarchy. 'The US should recognize that Vietnam is in a critical conditon and should treat it as a combat area of the cold war, as an area requiring immediate treatment.'

Reiterating the domino theory – Lansdale felt the South Vietnamese were the best defense against communism in Southeast Asia – he recommended across-the-board increases in American aid, strengthening the US-trained but still weak ARVN and fostering a positive coalition among Diem's non-communist loyal opposition, from whose ranks a successor to Diem would eventually emerge, and which would meanwhile add its energies in the struggle against communism. Almost the only positive aspect of the situation Lansdale found were some 'inspired counterguerrilla actions' taken by loyal paramilitary forces (Civil Guards and Self-Defense Corps) in highly localized areas. Also, while the number of insurgents and their control over the population had increased, the Vietcong (now numbering about 14,000 armed members) had neglected

Mao Tse-tung's cardinal tenet of sound political work at the grass-roots level. The people were under communist control, and unhappy about it, but 'too terrified to act.' Lansdale wrote, 'We still have a chance of beating them if we can give the people some fighting chance of gaining security and some political basis of action.'

Newly elected President John F Kennedy was particularly impressed with Lansdale's report on the counterproductive nature of US influence on Diem. So far, American pressure on Diem to enact essential reforms had only increased his intransigence and

Previous pages: South Vietnamese trainees watch intently as their comrades complete the obstacle course they have just finished at a US-run Regional Forces training center.
Top left: A US Special Forces civic-action team and its interpreter confer with a Muong chief about local conditions.

his reliance on his brother Nhu's implausible
schemes. Lansdale suggested that what America
needed was an 'unusual man' in Saigon who could
sympathize with Diem and nudge him in the right
direction. So impressed was Kennedy that he told
Lansdale he wanted him to go to Saigon as the new
ambassador. This idea shocked both Lansdale and
the State Department, which pointed out that in
terms of the kind of image the US wanted in Southeast Asia, the implications of sending a prominent
CIA agent on such a critical mission were
horrendous.

Counterinsurgency and Special Forces

Less than a month before Lansdale's trip to Viet-
nam, Hanoi had announced the formation of the
National Front for the Liberation of the South (the
NLF). Truly the Vietminh reborn, the NLF was a
broad yet communist-controlled coalition which
Diem's publicists, anxious to discredit the new
organization from the outset, quickly dubbed the
Vietcong (or Vietnamese Communists). And on 6

Above: *A member of the 1st
Special Forces Group at
Nai Ba Den instructs
Vietnamese volunteers in
use of the grenade.*
Opposite below: *A
youthful former Vietcong
joins American forces to
help them locate communist
positions.*

January 1961, while Lansdale was in Vietnam, Nikita Khrushchev announced that although the Soviet Union and other communist countries opposed both world and local wars, they approved of and supported 'just wars of liberation and popular uprisings.' His statement crystallized the communist position on 'Wars of National Liberation,' and made it clear that peoples emerging from colonialism had evolved a new kind of warfare.

American military thinking during the 1950s had centered on a vast European conventional World War III, in which critical terrain was lost or gained, and on a nuclear holocaust. But 'people's warfare' subordinated military action to political action, stressing the support of the indigenous population and the gain or loss of peoples' minds as the key to success. Addressing himself to this new brand of war, President Kennedy remarked to the 1962 West Point graduating class that new conditions of warfare required the buildup of a new force able to reach into conflicts where conventional armies were incapable of operating: 'This is another type of war, new in its intensity, ancient in its origins – war by guerrillas, subversives, insurgents, assassins; war by ambush instead of combat, by infiltration instead of aggression, seeking victory by eroding and exhausting the enemy instead of engaging him.' Unwilling to call this kind of war anything that

President John F Kennedy, a strong advocate of counterinsurgency tactics in Vietnam, confers with William Yarborough, Commandant of the US Special Warfare Center at Fort Bragg that now bears Kennedy's name.

smacked of the Spirit of '76 (the French, experienced in Algeria and Vietnam, called such conflicts Revolutionary War), Americans finally settled on 'Insurgency.' Counterinsurgency (COIN) thus emerged in the early days of Kennedy's New Frontier as the answer to communist expansion and the growing threats of subversion and wars of liberation.

One of Kennedy's first acts as President was to direct Secretary of Defense Robert McNamara to improve US capabilities for the conduct of paramilitary operations and unconventional war. In a special message to Congress, Kennedy said, 'We need a greater ability to deal with guerrilla forces, insurrection, and subversion, and we must help train local forces to be equally effective.' In March 1961 he asked Congress to provide the means to defeat 'small, externally supported bands of men.' Army Brigadier General William B Rosson, a veteran of Lansdale's SMM, was designated special assistant to the Army Chief of Staff for special warfare, and Kennedy favorite Marine Major General Victor Krulak became the first SACSA (Special Assistant for Counterinsurgency and Special Activities) to the Chairman of the Joint Chiefs of Staff, a Kennedy tribute to his understanding of the priority of political action in irregular warfare. Kennedy sent countless memorandums to the Pentagon and the Department of Defense to follow up his orders, and received countless proposals from such counterinsurgency theorists as Presidential Assistant Walt R Rostow, and Roger Hilsman of the State Department.

In April Kennedy approved a counterinsurgency plan for Vietnam which increased ARVN strength by 20,000 men, raised the Civil Guard strength to 68,000, upped Self-Defense Forces to 40,000 and improved ARVN elite forces. The South Vietnamese Ranger companies that had been added to each ARVN infantry battalion in 1960 were to receive improved training by US Special Forces at the Duc My Ranger School, established in 1961. In Laos, a MAAG was created, and the US White Star Special Forces teams were ordered to put on their uniforms and leave their CIA PEO cover. Counterinsurgency was on everyone's lips in Washington, and everyone – including the President – read Mao Tse-tung, Che Guevera and North Vietnam's General Giap, with varying degrees of comprehension. On 11 May 1961, President Kennedy ordered CIA Director Allen Dulles to organize a South Vietnamese unit for clandestine warfare in North Vietnam. On the same day, he approved sending 400 Special Forces troopers as well as 100 other American military advisors to South Vietnam to train the Vietnamese in counterinsurgency techniques, and in particular to work with the CIA on what at first was called the Tribal Area Development Program, then the Village Defense Program and finally the Civilian Irregular Defense Group (CIDG).

President Kennedy, while clearly the patron saint of counterinsurgency, is also considered by many, with some truth, as the patron saint of the Special Forces. Despite the US Army's traditional policy of avoiding political issues at home and abroad, he took the unusual step of arranging a private session with the Joint Chiefs of Staff to muster support for ambitious training programs at the Special Warfare

Above: *US Secretary of Defense Robert S McNamara (right) and General Lyman Lemnitzer, JCS Chairman (second from right) visit units of the US Military Assistance Command with American and Vietnamese officers – May 1962.*

Left: *An American advisor confers with a Vietnamese interpreter during allied operations in the Central Plateau region in 1964.*

Main picture: *A 1st Special Forces bunker on Nai Ba Den, showing sparsely settled and forested terrain typical of the Vietnam theater of war.*
Right: *A US Army Caribou supply plane makes a drop over the camp at Nai Ba Den.*
Far right: *US advisor Captain Roger Donlon discusses camp security at Nha Trang with ARVN Special Forces personnel. Donlon was the first American serviceman to win the Medal of Honor in Vietnam.*

Center at Fort Bragg, a facility he visited on 21 September 1961 and which now bears his name. Although the US Army has always looked with disfavor upon the concept of elite military organizations, Kennedy himself, as commander-in-chief, authorized the Special Forces to wear the unique headgear that became their symbol; a green beret rests to this day next to the eternal flame on his grave. Certainly, Kennedy perceived the Green Berets as the front line in counterinsurgency. But the basic objective of the Green Berets who arrived at Nha Trang in May and set up four remedial centers for training ARVN companies in combat skills and commando tactics (training 70 companies by late fall) had already changed from their original mission. Instead of waging guerrilla warfare against conventional forces in enemy territory (the role for which they were created), US Special Forces troopers in Vietnam were to find themselves attempting to thwart guerrilla insurgency in 'friendly' territory. Their role had become one of counter-insurgency.

The Special Forces trace their lineage back to the illustrious Rangers of World War II and to the 1st Special Forces Service, an elite force of three two-battalion regiments recruited in Canada and the United States in 1942, which served with legendary distinction in the Aleutians, North Africa, southern France and Italy (where it earned the nickname 'the Devil's Brigade'). The OSS, a hybrid with a strong political and intelligence flavor, also deserves a place as a legitimate ancestor of today's Green Berets. Such exploits as the training by OSS Detachment 101 of 11,000 Kachin tribesmen in northern Burma during World War II (who provided 90 percent of the intelligence in the theater and harassed the Japanese without ceasing) smacks of more recent Special Forces operations. But neither the 1st Special Service Force nor the OSS long survived World War II, and the elite US Ranger companies established during the Korean War were so woefully misdeployed that their potential was unrealized. Behind-the-lines activities by hastily improvised units in Korea also proved unsuccessful, although they served to teach the lesson that if special operations were to be carried out successfully, there would have to be preparation before the advent of a war. From these experiences, and the desire to develop guerrilla warfare plans for an anticipated World War III, the US Army reluctantly allotted 2500 personnel spaces to such a program. On 20 June 1952, the 10th Special Forces Group was activated at Fort Bragg Special Warfare Center, now the John F Kennedy Center of Military Assistance. The 77th Special Forces Group, the next unit formed, was activated at Fort Bragg on 25 September 1953.

Main picture: *The strategic hamlet program, here being implemented at Duc Toa, seemed a promising approach to village defense in the early 1960s. Too often, however, it resulted in a series of isolated enclaves surrounded by barbed wire and trenches and populated by resentful villagers who had been forced to relocate.*
Far left: *A US Advisors' compound in an ARVN village.*
Left: *The ARVN base camp at Hoi Vong Pass, safeguarding Route 1 north of Danang.*

On 24 June 1957 the 1st Special Forces Group, formed from a nucleus of two Special Forces detachments already sending training missions to Thailand, Taiwan and Vietnam from Japan and Hawaii, was activated on Okinawa. Shortly thereafter a team from this unit trained 58 ARVN at the Commando Training Center in Nha Trang. These troops became the instructors and cadre for the first Vietnamese Special Forces units (Lac Luong Dac Biet or LLDB, also known as VNSF). By this time US Special Forces were also acting as advisors to the Vietnamese Rangers and elite airborne units. In May 1960, in response to increased Vietcong activity, 30 Special Forces instructors left Fort Bragg to set up a training program for the South Vietnamese Army; later that year, more than 100 Green Berets under 'Bull' Simons arrived in Laos to train Meo tribesmen under the White Star program.

The basic operational unit of the Special Forces was the 12-man 'A-team,' a self-contained, self-sustaining group trained to survive and to operate with a minimum of outside assistance in any environment from the Arctic to the tropics. The A-team normally consisted of a commanding officer, usually a captain; an executive officer, usually a lieutenant; an operations sergeant; an intelligence sergeant; a heavy weapons leader; a light weapons leader; a medical specialist; a radio operator specialist; an engineer sergeant; a chief of research and development operator; an assistant medical specialist; and an engineer assistant. Two men each were allotted to the medical and engineering specialities because they were considered particularly important in winning the trust of indigenous minorities with civic-action projects; languages were taught, and each man was cross-trained in at least one other function so that skills were duplicated in case the team was split or suffered casualties.

By 21 September 1961, when the 5th Special Forces Group of 1st Special Forces – which eventually took charge of all SF operations in Vietnam – was activated at Fort Bragg, overall strength stood at about 2000 extremely well-trained men. They comprised three Special Forces Groups – the 10th in Germany, the 77th at Fort Bragg and the 1st on Okinawa. President Kennedy increased Special-Forces numbers fourfold, viewing the Green Berets as the prime instrument of counterinsurgency, a role no one in the US military establishment had considered before. Early in 1962, when the US Government began setting up the interdepartmental machinery for aiding South Vietnam, it was inevitable that the Green Berets, trained specifically for unconventional warfare, would play a conspicuous role.

Although perhaps best prepared, the Army was not the only arm of service equipped to supply counterinsurgency teams. By this time, counterinsurgency had developed almost a fad status in Washington, and the Navy was able to contribute SEAL (sea, air, land) units trained to parachute into the sea with scuba gear, and to emerge from the water ready to fight. Navy Regulus missile-carrying submarines were converted to carry troops, and miniature four-man submarines were prepared for sea infiltration. The Air Force Air Commandos, with Australian-style bush hats and rapid-fire Armalite rifles, included some of the hottest pilots in the Air Force, flying modified and aging T-6, T-28, C-47, World War II B-26, Naval Corsair, and Army Caribou C-123 transport propeller planes. The Special Forces considered the Air Commandos their blood brothers, whose timely intervention often saved the day in Vietnam, and Air Force FACs (Forward Air Controllers) lived in many Special Forces camps and performed flawless aerial reconnaissance. In April 1961, 350 Air Commandos were

Main picture: *A
Montagnard crew fires its
106-mm recoilless rifle at
suspected enemy positions
near Camp Bu Prang.*
Inset: *The 5th Special
Forces Group evolved from
1st Special Forces in
September 1961 to train
South Vietnamese
popular forces.*

organized into the 4400th Combat Crew Training Squadron, better known as 'Jungle Jim,' which taught Vietnamese flyers the counterinsurgency techniques of interdiction, air reconnaissance and ground support. Provided a South Vietnamese pilot-trainee was aboard, Jungle Jim was authorized to fly combat missions, called training missions under the code name FARMGATE, often in support of Special Forces and CIDG operations. In June 1963, the 4400th was redesignated the 1st Air Commando Squadron, and was joined in October 1964 by a second FARMGATE squadron, the 602nd, both of which were now equipped with powerful A-1E fighter-bombers.

The 67-man 507th Tactical Control Group, an Air Force combat reporting group and nucleus of a tactical air control support system, preceded Jungle Jim to Vietnam, arriving covertly in September of 1960 with all insignia and identification marks on their equipment painted out. Special warfare, employing new technologies, developed along with counterinsurgency forces; this was, of course, the first helicopter war. Under the auspices of the Department of Defense, a Combat Development and Test Center was established in Vietnam to explore ways to weaken the insurgents through such area-denial schemes as large-scale 'weather-modification techniques,' as well as more down-to-earth methods involving the use of napalm and chemical agents to destroy Vietcong cover and indigenous food supplies, tapioca in particular. In February 1962, a 69-man USAF Special Area Spray Flight unit began Defoliation Operation Ranch Hand: eventually, millions of gallons of herbicides containing chemical agents including one dioxin – so-called Agent Orange – were dropped over 10–20 percent of Vietnam. In February 1962, the USAF suffered its first casualties of the war when one of its C-123s equipped with tanks and sprayers crashed into the jungle. The US Army's 23rd Special Air Warfare

Main picture: *Ground crews load rocket launchers on T-28 aircraft at Bien Hoa Airbase, watched by Vietnamese Air Force personnel and US Air Commandos.*
Opposite top: *Two US Special Forces advisors check perimeter defenses of a South Vietnamese village in 1964.*
Above: *A US advisor removes a bazooka shell that had been wrongly inserted.*

Detachment, flying OV-1 turboprop Mohawks armed with .50-caliber machine guns and cameras, performed visual and photographic reconnaissance to position insurgents for ARVN ground units. A little-known group of professional irregulars, the Australian Special Air Service (ASAS), the first of whom arrived in 1962 to train Vietnamese in jungle warfare, fought alongside the Green Berets from 1963 onward, advising ARVN Rangers and leading CIDG units.

Civilian Irregular Defense Group

CIDG, a CIA-sponsored pilot program designed to mobilize indigenous minorities to mount their own counterinsurgency effort, became the chief work of the Special Forces in the Vietnam war. Although a relatively small operation in the overall context of the war, it was the largest, most innovative and most

Main picture:
Montagnard *Commandos*
fire carbines on the rifle
range at the Pleiyit
Commando Training
Center in 1963.
Inset: *Trainees for the*
Montagnard *Commandos*
prepare their weapons and
supplies for a patrol into
Vietcong territory.

effective unconventional allied warfare program in the theater. Inspired by French success in mobilizing *Montagnard* guerrilla units against the Vietminh, and CIA success with Meo tribesmen in Laos, the CIDG program was based on a realistic assessment of the counterinsurgency potential of the 700,000 aboriginal tribesmen who inhabited over 75 percent of Vietnam's rugged mountain interior. (The remaining 14 million Vietnamese were jammed into the fertile deltas and narrow coastal lowlands). These *Montagnards* were, by-and-large, unaware that there was a country called Vietnam. They and the other minorities of the interior were neither pro-communist, pro-Vietcong, nor pro-government; they knew nothing to be pro about, and followed a traditional way of life. The CIA concept was that if they were given something to fight for and with, they would fight to maintain their peace and security, which was gradually being eroded by the Vietcong because of the strategic importance of their territory; and that in so fighting they would commit themselves against the communists and in support of the government of South Vietnam.

The authors of the CIDG program studied Vo Nguyen Giap's book of operating principles, which the Vietcong appeared to be following to the letter. They decided to use these proven principles against the Vietcong and to reinforce their application with better support, better organization and sincerity of purpose. In practice, there was considerable improvisation, as the CIDG program developed according to the methods found necessary to identify the enemy to the tribes. In the conduct of the program over more than nine years, the Special Forces became involved in almost every conceivable aspect of counterinsurgency – except for political indoctrination.

The prototype of the CIDG effort was among the Rhade, one of the largest tribes of *Montagnards* – probably the largest single minority – and the least primitive, in the village of Buon Enao in Darlac province. A two-week visit by a CIA agent and a Special Forces medical specialist to the village in October 1961 resulted in a promise to participate from the villagers, many of whom supported the Vietcong out of fear but also resented the government for withdrawing medical and educational projects. A fence was built around the village, both to provide security and to demonstrate participation in the program, and shelters were dug inside the village where women and children could take refuge in case of attack. The villagers pledged publicly that no Vietcong would enter their village or receive assistance of any kind; on 15 December 1961 the first 50 weapons – Swedish 'K' submachine guns – were issued to the first 50 volunteers.

At a meeting in January between South Vietnamese Government officials, Rhade tribal leaders and the CIA, the Rhade agreed to denounce the Vietcong and to support the government of South Vietnam, provided the government did not participate in the expansion of the program. Mutual alienation was almost complete between the highlanders and the lowlanders; the ethnic Vietnamese traditionally called the Montagnards *moi*, or 'savages,' and candidly considered them an inferior people, annexing their tribal lands and denying them the benefits supplied to other citizens. One of the great incentives for the *Montagnards* to join the program was the understanding that if they controlled Vietcong activity in their territory, ARVN troops would no longer have any excuse to cross their lands. The Vietnamese were unhappy about the program, particularly about plans to arm the villagers, but they agreed to let the Americans run it. The CIA then called in the Special Forces, and on 13 February 1962 seven Green Berets under Captain Ron Shackleton (one-half of an A-team, Detachment A-113) flew to Vietnam to join CIA advisors and 10 Vietnamese Special Forces (half of whom were always *Montagnards*) at Buon Enao. Their task in the Village Defense Program, as it was then called, was to recruit and train a small paid 'strike force' which would defend the village in case of attack, reinforce a threatened area, patrol between villages, gather intelligence and set ambushes. The Special Forces then trained a second group of unpaid 'village defenders,' in the rudiments of small-arms operations and village defense, and supplied them with a radio with which to call for help. This force lived and worked in the village, fighting only in self-defense. Civic actions and psychological operations (psy ops) – digging wells, airlifting elephants, taking amazed tribesmen on junkets to Danang – were part of the Special Forces mission from the start, and were well received by a people accustomed to abuse and neglect. As originally conceived, the Village Defense Program was in fact a massive civic-action program, and at this point, as far as Special Forces counter-insurgency theory was concerned, counterguerrilla combat operations were only the military part of the solution.

Medical treatment in particular often opened the way to friendly contact with the population. After the tribesmen had had a chance to observe the benefits of medical service, they were told that they could build their own dispensary if they were willing to defend it by fencing their village and providing young men to protect it. If they did, the Special Forces would provide medicines, train a local medic and extend the area of strike-force operations to include their village. Hundreds of volunteer villages came into the program this way.

Despite initial Vietcong attacks, the program expanded rapidly. The Rhade response to the program was positive and encouraging, and the people proved they were willing and able to defend themselves, their homes and families against any aggressor, without support from conventional ARVN forces. The combination of armed villagers experiencing an improvement in their lives and constantly patrolling strike forces was consistently successful, and as word spread, more and more people asked to be made part of the program. Its basic strength was that it left in place a loyal population that successfully reported and resisted insurgent activities on its home ground. The Special Forces found from the first that the hold of the Vietcong was weak and existed mainly because local Vietnamese officials had nothing better to offer.

By the time Shackleton and his team completed their six-month tour in August, Buon Enao had become a base center for the surrounding villages, and the program was well underway with 1800 men in the strike force, 280 trained medics and 129 Rhade hamlets protected by close to 10,000 village

defenders. By the end of 1962, there were 12 A-teams in Vietnam; by early 1963 the program had secured several hundred villages, 300,000 civilians and several thousand square miles of territory from the Vietcong, utilizing 38,000 armed civilian irregulars. In many areas, Vietcong presence was practically eliminated, and the Special Forces had unquestionably gained the respect and affection of the minorities. In the remote *Montagnard* territories of Vietnam in the early 1960s, Special Forces CIDG camps were virtually the only government presence, the only expanding islands of security and the only sources of intelligence. By the end of 1963, more than 65,000 militiamen and strike-force members were trained by the Special Forces. A year later, out of necessity, the 5th Special Forces Group was activated specifically for duty in Vietnam, with 45 A-teams controlled by five B-teams, which in turn were controlled by two C-teams.

The concept of local defense with roving strike forces worked not only with the *Montagnards*, but with Diem's Republican and Catholic Youth paramilitary groups, with Father Hoa and his Chinese refugees and in such groups as the 'fighting fathers,'

Above: *View from an H-21 helicopter of a typical* Montagnard *resettlement area: fortified villages were manned by mountaineers trained to defend themselves against communist guerrillas.*

Opposite: *CIDG soldiers on the perimeter of their camp at Duc Co, one wearing camouflage jacket and the other 'black-pajama' guerrilla garb used by indigenous soldiers of both sides.*

in which Catholic parish priests encouraged Special Forces training and arming of their parishioners. The Village Defense Program, of course, spread to other tribes – the Jarai and the Mnongs – with notable failures among the Katu and the Bahnar, who proved too few, too suspicious and too backward to organize. Even such dubiously motivated Cambodian groups as the Khmer Serei and the Khmer Kampuchea Krom (KKK) and the ethnic Chinese Nungs became involved. Eventually, the CIDG program expanded to include the remnants of the private armies of the Cao Dai and the Hoa Hao religious sects of the Mekong Delta, which had once violently opposed President Diem, and whose goals, like those of the *Montagnards* and other groups who came under the CIDG umbrella, were not always the same as those of the government. Moving away from the strictly defensive posture of village security, the CIDG program eventually emerged as an amalgamation of many small programs, all of which aimed at the protection and development of minority groups against insurgency, with a total of 75,000 armed irregulars in 1964.

Shortly after the experiment at Buon Enao began, Special Forces started training paramilitary units at the Hoa Cam Training Center in Danang, using *Montagnard* recruits. Later known as Mountain Scouts, these irregulars (originally CIA-sponsored) undertook long-range missions in remote mountain and jungle areas, to provide government presence and to gather intelligence. Special Forces were also the cadre for the Trailwatchers program, later known as Border Surveillance units, whose task was to identify and report Vietcong movements near the border in their area, and to capture or destroy Vietcong units when possible. Special Forces also participated in such CIA operations as the Combat Intelligence Teams (650 men) and the Civilian Airborne Rangers (450 men), which performed covert intelligence and sabotage missions in Laos and Cambodia, and were eventually militarized and absorbed into the LLDB. On 1 November 1963, when transfer of the border surveillance units and the mountain scouts from CIA to Department of Defense control (under CIDG) was completed, total personnel in both groups numbered about 8000.

By all accounts, the CIDG program, as it was formally named after Buon Enao, was an outstanding success until the spring of 1963. At this time it was removed from CIA control and turned over to the US military under Operation SWITCHBACK, a global divestment of larger CIA paramilitary operations caused by President Kennedy's dissatisfaction with the Bay of Pigs debacle. Also official Vietnamese support for the program, which had always ranged from passive to violent opposition, became increasingly questionable, culminating in demands to disarm the *Montagnards*.

SWITCHBACK was completed on 1 July 1963. Its completion and the transfer of the CIDG program exclusively to military hands corresponded with the increased tempo of infiltration and of the war in general. The village-defender idea faded as the CIDG program took on a more military and aggressive orientation. At the same time, because of its success, it expanded throughout Vietnam at a rapid pace, perhaps too rapidly to allow for the careful site selection and civic nurturing the program demanded. And the conventionalization of CIDG forces began, along with the turnover of established CIDG camps to Vietnamese Special Forces control. Officially, by 1964, US Special Forces were given the mission of 'border surveillance,' and camps were established on the borders

Above: *A Ranger Long-Range Reconnaissance Patrol team in action.*

Right: *CIDG trainees under command of Vietnamese Special Forces*

personnel fire M-79 grenade launchers as a Green Beret advisor looks on.

A C-ration lunch.

for purely military objectives; they were staffed by *Montagnards* recruited from more populous or civilized areas. The CIDG concept evolved into one where an A-team moved into a border area, built a sort of frontier fort and moved in three to five strike-force companies (now standardized at 150 men each) to defend the camp and secure the surrounding area. The political underpinning and territorial integrity of the program were lost, and its original efficiency, at least for a time, was diminished. The bulk of CIDG camps established in 1964 were placed along the Cambodian-Laotian border, to counter infiltration. By July 1964, CIDG strike-force troops were manning 24 border camps, and the emphasis had definitely shifted from creating defense systems for existing villages, with priority on civil action, to using newly established CIDG villages as bases for offensive strike-force 'VC Hunter' counterguerrilla warfare. CIDG strike forces were also increasingly employed with regular government troops in joint operations for which they were generally neither trained nor equipped. By December 1963, 18,000 men had been trained as strike-force troops and 43,376 as hamlet militia (village defenders). But the Special Forces assumption of the border surveillance mission and the de-emphasis of area development eventually resulted in the training of strike-

force troops only. Few hamlet militia were trained after November 1963, and almost none after April 1964.

From its earliest operations, the US Special-Forces concept had always been to let the indigenous people do the job; Vietnamization, introduced as a new concept in 1969, had been the basis for the CIDG program from 1962. Once an area was considered secure, it was to be turned over to provincial control. Following SWITCHBACK, Buon Enao was turned over, but the dismal failure of this operation graphically demonstrated many of the problems of institutional Vietnamese control, which eventually resulted in a *Montagnard* uprising.

At Buon Enao, the government was unprepared at every level to take over and continue area development, and the people, especially the strike-force troops, already irritated and confused by Saigon's demands to repossess their weapons, had little interest in being absorbed into conventional Vietnamese units. Buon Enao had served as a symbol for the whole program; once in Vietnamese hands, according to a Special-Forces report, 'Enao complex was disorganized and most of its effectiveness had been lost.' Dispensary facilities were dismantled and moved, strike-force troops and village health workers went without pay for months and

'Tiger-suited' Vietnamese
members of a Special
Forces Strike Team confer
with a village chief and his
assistant (lower left).

two-thirds of the 900-man strike force was scattered by the Vietnamese province chief on various operations. Friction between lowland Vietnamese Special Forces and the *Montagnards* they commanded had sometimes erupted into fighting, and in September 1964 bad feeling between the Vietnamese and the *Montagnards* – who still had no vote, no secure ownership of their land, no representation in government, no courts, no regional autonomy, and basically no rights at all under the government they fought for – resulted in co-ordinated armed uprisings. Five CIDG camps in II Corps Tactical Zone were affected; at Buong Brieng, Ban Don, Bu Prang, Buon Sar Pa and Buon Mi Ga.

The uprising was undoubtedly not without the influence of FULRO (Force of the Unification of the Oppressed Races), a *Montagnard* nationalist organization led by Y-Bham which considered *any* Vietnamese an enemy and an obstacle to the goal of *Montagnard* autonomy. Twenty-six LLDB were killed, and others held captive, together with several hundred Vietnamese civilians and several US Special-Forces advisors. With CIDG troops advancing on provincial capital Ban Me Thuot, the situation was ripe for a bloodbath; 17 Vietnamese Popular-Force soldiers and two Vietnamese civilians were also killed. Fortunately, US Special-

Forces advisors, drawing upon the reservoir of good will they had built up among the Rhade, managed, by wringing some concessions to *Montagnard* nationalism from the government, to bring the rebellion under control and end it. At a conference in Pleiku from 15-17 October, Vietnamese officials listened to *Montagnard* demands, agreed to some and promised to study others.

One of the principal sources of friction between the *Montagnards* and the Vietnamese was the presence of LLDB in the CIDG program. Technically, the LLDB directed CIDG operations. Although the ultimate goal of the program was indigenous leadership upon the departure of both US and Vietnamese Special Forces, Vietnamese policy forbade CIDG leaders above the company level, which effectively prevented the training of indigenous leaders. In fact, lack of rapport between LLDB and *Montagnards*, as well as a provision called Parasol Switchback, which gave the US Special Forces continuing financial responsibility for the program, left the Green Berets in effective control. There was, however, a certain logic for the presence of LLDB in the program despite their generally negative effect. Both the LLDB and the CIDG were CIA projects from the start. As many CIA members were former Green Berets, USSF

US Marines and ARVN soldiers join forces in an area search for Vietcong who have established themselves in nearby wooded hills.

detachments had been used for training in both cases.

After the 1954 Geneva Accords, when US aid to Vietnam became direct and began its long spiral upward, the Special Forces had helped build a Vietnamese special-forces offensive warfare capability. Emphasis was not on counterinsurgency at the time; 1st Special Forces Group troopers were teaching ambushing at Nha Trang in 1957. Also in the late 1950s, a team from the 77th Special Forces began training the prototype of the ARVN Rangers, a highly successful program expanded by President Kennedy which produced some of the best ARVN infantry units, much feared by the Vietcong. The Rangers at one time even had their own hit song, the Vietnamese equivalent to the 'Ballad of the Green Berets.'

Vietnamese Elite Forces

The Vietnamese Special Forces were organized by the CIA in 1956, under the name of the 1st Observation Battalion. They were not an official part of the Vietnamese Armed Forces, but operated directly under the Presidential Survey Office (PSO). Under their commander, Colonel Tung, they en-joyed the very special status of palace guards (the LLDB were understandably unpopular with regular ARVN), and were always available for special details dreamed up by President Diem and his brother, Nhu. Following the aborted 1962 coup, Diem always kept at least 600 LLDB and the 4800-man Airborne Brigade under his personal control, as 'coup insurance.' On 21 August 1963, Nhu and Diem, in an attempt to neutralize two blocs of their most potent non-communist adversaries, the Buddhists and the Army, by turning them against each other, had the LLDB dress as regular ARVN soldiers and attack Buddhist temples, pagodas and sanctuaries in Saigon, Hué and other cities, destroying property and beating and arresting numerous monks, nuns, students, activists and ordinary citizens.

The scheme did not work. Most of Diem's staunchest American supporters – including President Kennedy – now turned against him, and the Army generals redoubled efforts to mount a coup against Diem. John F Kennedy's ambassador in Saigon, Henry Cabot Lodge, encouraged the administration to support the dissident generals in their coup attempt, and CIA operative Lucien Conein began meeting with dissident general Duong

Van Minh, assuring him that the US would not thwart a coup and would continue economic and military aid. Conein monitored rebel activity through clandestine meetings with General Tran Van Dong (some in a dentist's office). The self-immolation of several Buddhist monks in protest of Diem's policies, and fresh reports of intensified political repression, including the arrest of scores of children, led the United States, fed up with the use of LLDB for political purposes, to announce on 21 October 1963 that it would deny funds to the Vietnamese Special Forces if they were used for anything other than fighting the Vietcong. By now coup plans were well advanced, and Diem's brother Nhu had generated elaborate plans for his own pre-emptive pseudo-coup, in which a rebellion would for a few days appear to succeed, only to be crushed by the timely arrival of Colonel Tung and his LLDB. By this strategy he hoped to impress the Americans with his ability to subdue a 'pro-communist' challenge to his government, and draw out real coup plotters so they could be arrested.

Both Nhu and Diem, thanks to their network of spies, knew the real coup was due around 1 November, but thought they had matters well in hand. The US also knew, and only the dissident generals, still

awaiting some final sign of American approval, remained uncertain. When they got their signal and the coup proceeded, Conein monitored the event from the rebel Joint General Staff headquarters, transmitting updates to Ambassador Lodge, and supplying cash to compensate families of troops killed in the coup. Among the generals' first victims were Colonel Tung and his brother (second in command of the LLDB), who were brought to the JGS headquarters and shot. Nhu and Diem were also killed, although this was not part of the American plan. With Diem, Nhu and Tung out of the way, the LLDB officially became part of the Vietnamese armed forces; the new LLDB dated itself from 1963. Its palace guard missions were over, but suspicion and lack of support within the Vietnamese Army remained as its legacy, and hampered its efforts to obtain high-quality personnel.

The Vietnamese Marine Corps also participated in the coup that overthrew Diem, but quickly returned to fighting communists. Diem himself had created the VNMC in October 1954, drawing its first members from former elite assault troops and French-trained Army and Navy commandos. The VNMC proved itself in combat against the Hoa Hao in the Mekong Delta in 1955, and grew until it

A member of the Vietnamese National Police Field Force outside the CHAM Museum in Danang.

reached a strength of two landing battalions of 728 men each the following year. By the end of 1958, the 1st Battalion was conducting platoon and company-sized operations against insurgents in the swamps of An Xuyen province, where it soon earned the Marines a reputation as one of the most effective Vietnamese Armed Forces units. The VNMC, along with the ARVN Airborne Brigade, was designated the general-reserve force for the Vietnamese Armed Forces, and at the time of the coup had become a 6109-man brigade. Throughout the years following the coup, the VNMC continued in the forefront of counterinsurgency activities, reaching divisional size (as did the ARVN airborne forces) by 1970.

Among the many ethnic groups the US Special Forces worked with during this period, the Nungs, a tribe from northern Vietnam which served under the French and migrated to the Central Highlands in 1954, proved to be particularly adept fighters. Ethnic Chinese with a mercenary military tradition, the Nungs entered into contracts with the Green Berets as a special security strike force when the CIDG program expanded in 1964-5, and were directly responsible to them. Among the exploits which earned them this special status was their role in the defense of CIDG camp Nam Dong. Its 300-man strike force was attacked by several hundred Vietcong on 6 July 1964, beginning with a heavy mortar barrage at 2:30 AM that caused 80 percent of the strike-force casualties in the first 15 minutes, and utterly destroyed the radio shack, the dispensary and the Nung barracks. But the Nungs, who had sensed something coming, were all armed, alert and at their posts. Under the direction of Special Forces Detachment commander Captain Roger H C Donlon, they managed to hang onto the camp by sheer will; the Vietnamese district chief waited until daylight to send two Civil Guard companies to relieve them. Donlon himself was painfully wounded in the stomach, shoulder, leg and face, but continued for five hours to rally the defenders, surviving the fight to win the first Medal of Honor in Vietnam.

Nam Dong took place before the existence of the crack 'Mike' mobile reaction forces of future years. Other CIDG camps, isolated by their very nature, were not as lucky as Nam Dong. The interim period before the massive buildup of conventional US forces in Vietnam in 1965 was rough going for counterinsurgency border surveillance, which, with Vietcong operations intensifying almost daily, was given top priority and particular Special-Forces attention. With the shift in emphasis accompanying SWITCHBACK, the newly established CIDG camps near the border tended to be too far apart; while they were located in areas of strategic importance, the population was often too sparse to afford adequate recruits, and consequently the deep motivation of troops defending their own ground was lacking. Typically, a new border surveillance camp engaged and inflicted casualties on the Vietcong for a few weeks, then lapsed into inertia. There was no interlocking patrol pattern between border surveillance camps, and the Vietnamese Special Forces were unwilling to carry out offensive operations with civilian irregulars, viewing the operation as an American project.

Arguing that the *Montagnards* lacked trained leaders, the LLDB consistently resisted patroling in squads and platoons; of course, it was this group's refusal to allow leadership training for irregulars which created the lack of leaders. Consequently, patrols were generally of company size and carried out in daylight. Although in a few cases *Montagnards* were deservedly commissioned as officers in the LLDB, and although not all LLDB were short-sighted, command problems inevitably arose when any Vietnamese was placed between the USSF and the indigenous forces. While the LLDB were nominally the strike-force commanders in camp and on operations, on patrol they often simply abdicated this role. The Green Berets took up the slack, but this wasn't enough. As a result, the border surveillance camps had no real success in controlling enemy movements across the border; matériel and personnel flow were acknowledged by all hands to be subject to increase at the enemy's will. As American military involvement increased, so did the number of men and supplies moving down the Ho Chi Minh Trail.

Above: *The riverine war along South Vietnam's numerous waterways involved both popular civilian forces like these soldiers and US Special Forces including Navy SEALs. This photograph was taken aboard a US Navy River Patrol Boat en route to a night ambush position on the Vinh Te Canal.*

Left: *Allied forces on the lookout for fishing boats that could be smuggling arms into South Vietnam – April 1965.*

Covert War: 1961-66

Previous pages: *An SP-SM Marlin Seaplane on Market Time operations in 1965.*

Opposite: *A Laotian soldier practices cover and concealment under supervision of US White Star teams, which dropped their PEO cover in 1961 and came into the open under orders from President Kennedy. The impetus was increasing communist infiltration through the permeable Laotian frontier.*

Above: *'Tunnel rats' on a search mission uncover training aids used to teach Vietcong recruits how to install and camouflage booby traps.*

Following pages: *A Navy SEAL team operating with Commander Task Force 116 leaves its Binh Thuy base for a night operation in the Mekong Delta.*

Part of John F Kennedy's May 1961 expansion of American involvement in the Vietnam War included a top-secret order to organize a clandestine war against North Vietnam. The chosen instruments for conducting secret warfare were the Central Intelligence Agency and the new Cold-War shock troops, the Green Berets. Some of the 400 Special Forces advisors sent to Vietnam would concentrate on training the embryonic Vietnamese Special Forces, which soon included a clandestine arm known as the Special Branch for highly classified missions.

Covert Action: The Lansdale Legacy

President Kennedy also directed the CIA to expand ARVN's 1st Observation Group from 340 to over 800 members, with training assistance from US Special Forces. The mission of these South Vietnamese agents was to form resistance networks, establish bases in North Vietnam and conduct light harassment. The 1st Observation Group was augmented by a special Vietnamese Air Force Transport Squadron – commanded by a young ace pilot named Nguyen Cao Ky – flying old C-47s, which dropped agents by parachute into North Vietnam in an operation code-named HAYLIFT. Another group of 450 CIA-trained Civilian Airborne Rangers were organized to perform covert raids in North Vietnam and Laos, as well as special intelligence and security operations in South Vietnam. US Green Berets and US Navy SEALs taught the Vietnamese agents special land and sea infiltration tactics.

In October 1961, Kennedy expanded covert missions for South Vietnamese agents directed at North

Vietnamese infiltration operations in the Laotian panhandle, while approving for the first time participation of US advisors 'as necessary.' Some Vietnam-based Americans did see action in Laos as a result of these early 'over-the-fence' (cross-border) operations. Missions included infiltration of agents under light civilian cover to locate and attack communist bases and lines of communication. A few months earlier, during the March 1961 Laos Crisis, Kennedy had ordered 107 US Special Forces White Star advisors to shed their 'PEO' cover, put on uniforms and begin similar anti-communist operations with Meo and Kha tribesmen in Laos.

The object of these covert 'harassment' operations was to put pressure on North Vietnam to cease its subversive insurgency against the South. Subversion of the North was never US policy. Kennedy sought to use unconventional warfare (in conjunction with diplomacy) as a policy instrument that, when necessary, could turn up the heat on Hanoi and demonstrate US capability to foment insurgency in North Vietnam and interdict, if necessary, the infiltration/supply lines in Laos. But Kennedy feared sending conventional American forces into the wild, rugged terrain of Laos. This reluctance stemmed from President Eisenhower's private warning to JFK (19 January 1961) that he might soon have to send troops into Laos. During the Laos Crisis in March 1961, the US Joint Chiefs told Kennedy that it would be easy to send several American divisions into Laos; extracting them might be a different story, requiring escalation and, perhaps, the JCS warned, use of tactical nuclear weapons. Shortly thereafter, Kennedy agreed with the Soviet Union to a second Geneva Conference – this time aimed at neutralization of Laos – in the hope that a treaty enforced by the two superpowers

could shield South Vietnam from Northern infiltration via Laos. However, few top-level American decision-makers – caught up in fighting wars of national liberation – realized that the commitment of Ho Chi Minh's 'unification struggle' transcended America's limited goals, and 'pin-prick' covert methods.

American-backed attempts to organize resistance networks duplicated Lansdale's old SMM Binh effort, which had proved unsuccessful in 1954. Dropping agents into North Vietnam brought few dividends; North Vietnamese captured many teams soon after infiltration and caught others trying to make their escape after aborted missions. Captured agents were thoroughly interrogated and served as useful communist propaganda weapons to denounce American and South Vietnamese violations of the 1954 Geneva Agreements.

At the same time, North Vietnamese activity in Laos increased dramatically. NVA and Pathet Lao forces, aided by Soviet military supplies dropped by Russian transport aircraft, pushed Royal Lao troops out of the Laotian panhandle, often with North Vietnamese 'advisors' urging unaggressive Pathet Lao troops forward at gunpoint. North Vietnam's goal was not a 'military takeover' of Laos, but rather quiet consolidation over the strategic trails and access routes into South Vietnam. Hanoi hoped to accomplish this without triggering American intervention. Control over those trails could turn the entire war into a simple battle of logistics, with the flow of men and matériel down the Trail determining the pace and scope of combat in the South.

The task of tackling North Vietnamese infiltration via Laos fell to the secret American-trained guerrilla armies operating on shoestring budgets. The full extent of NVA involvement was reported early by CIA-backed Meo guerrillas, who uncovered evidence of dog meat in vacated Pathet Lao camps (no self-respecting Lao ate dog meat, but Vietnamese did). These native guerrilla units also tracked and harassed NVA infiltration lines. But veteran unconventional warriors realized the only way to save South Vietnam was by a committed effort – a 'full court press' – to close down the infiltration pipeline in Laos. Since Kennedy had closed off the conventional military option, many believed an unconventional effort could achieve the desired results, more quietly and at much lower cost.

Briefly in 1961, Lt Colonel Arthur 'Bull' Simons believed that the United States might have checked large-scale communist infiltration in the Bolovens Plateau, the southern extension of the Ho Chi Minh Trail that emptied into the porous South Vietnamese border at thousands of points.

Simons, the first White Star commander in 1959, returned in 1961 for a second tour, this time out from under the PEO 'cover.' Bull Simons proved to be no ordinary military advisor, but the prototype unconventional soldier of the Vietnam War: rugged and brave, but not full of bravado; a meticulous planner who left nothing to chance and did not take foolish risks with his men. Throughout his military career, beginning as an ROTC artillery officer in 1941, Simons had demonstrated that rare quality in combat: initiative under fire. As a company commander of the 6th Ranger Battalion, Simons had led daring raids against Japanese radar installations

before the 1944 Leyte Gulf invasion. He joined Fort Bragg's old 77th Special Forces Group in the 1950s, and was chosen to lead the first clandestine White Star mission into Laos in 1959. From that point on, much of the 'Bull Simons story' is surrounded by legend.

Simons and his 107 Special-Forces troops arrived in Laos to find few Lao military units worthy of combat, so the American officer combed the Lao countryside kidnapping thousands of Meo tribesmen. In a short time, he had trained, clothed and fed 12 battalions of combat-effective troops to fight the Pathet Lao and NVA. At one point, one of these units defected to the Pathet Lao, taking their US Special-Force advisors prisoner. Simons reportedly helicoptered into the battalion's compound, confronted the commander and threatened to call in an airstrike on his troops unless the advisors were released. After Simons left with the Americans, he called in the airstrike anyway. Completing his six-month tour, Simons brought back every one of his troops alive. 'I would follow Bull Simons to hell and back,' one soldier remembered, 'for the sheer joy of being with him on the visit.'

Returning in mid-1961, Simons launched a new recruiting campaign among the Kha tribes on the Bolovens Plateau. In a scant six months, 60 Green Beret advisors from Simons' teams organized over 600 Kha tribesmen and virtually cleared the Bolovens Plateau of Pathet Lao. Although not as aggressive as the Meo, the Kha soldiers, when well led, motivated and fighting on home turf, were formidable. Simons hoped to organize another 10,000 Kha guerrillas and start to clear the Lao-South Vietnamese border areas before *Doan 559* tightened its grip on the Laotian panhandle.

However, the United States signed the Geneva Accords in July 1962, which 'neutralized' Laos and required withdrawal of all American and North Vietnamese advisors. Simons' White Star teams were checked out of Laos by International Control Commission (ICC) observers and not allowed to return. Since the Kha program was an all-Special-

Above: *South Vietnamese soldiers moving along the Ho Chi Minh Trail in Laos. During the period of US involvement, the trail became the principal communist supply and infiltration route, as security tightened along the coastlines.*

Opposite: *A Vietnamese infantryman who knows where his next meal is coming from – 1962.*

Above: *The Vietnamese Air Force pledges loyalty to President Ngo Dinh Diem in Saigon after a political uprising and assassination attempt (March 1962).*

Forces project (not CIA), the promising Kha guerrilla force languished and died. However, an estimated 10,000 North Vietnames troops did not leave Laos. ICC representatives formally witnessed the ceremonial departure of a mere 40 NVA soldiers, leading one American to remark that even these 40 communists probably sneaked back over the border a few miles downstream.

Soon after the Geneva Accords were signed, Hanoi ordered *Doan 559* to develop a mechanized transport capacity and new trail routes on an 'urgent' basis. Older routes were apparently deemed too vulnerable to interdiction by unconventional troops like the Kha and the Meo. *Doan 559's* mission remained simple: keep open an unimpeded route to funnel men and matériel into South Vietnam.

When Kennedy discovered that the North Vietnamese were flagrantly violating the 1962 accords, he angrily authorized stepped-up covert activities in Laos. The CIA Meo program (which had remained intact) was ordered onto the offensive against the North Vietnamese, while Lao, Meo and mercenary pilots began flying clandestine T-28 airstrikes against the Ho Chi Minh Trail. This was the origin of the controversial 'secret air war in Laos,' which later caused a Congressional outcry upon publication of the *Pentagon Papers* in 1971. These early top-secret operations, undertaken at the request of Premier Souvanna Phouma's neutralist Lao

Government, remained tightly restricted and controlled by the US Embassy in Vientiane, to maintain at least the facade of American adherence to the 1962 Geneva Agreement. The Meo and T-28 strikes remained 'plausibly deniable' activities.

Forfeiting the option of full-blown unconventional warfare in Laos forced Kennedy to raise the stakes in South Vietnam. By the end of 1962, over 11,000 US military advisors were in the field training the increasingly hard-pressed conventional ARVN. At the time of Kennedy's death in November 1963, the number of Americans in uniform in South Vietnam had grown to over 16,000.

CIA's Far-Flung Paramilitary Empire

The CIA's covert activities covered all of Southeast Asia – from village defense in the CIDG and secret

Civilian Airborne Rangers in South Vietnam, to the Meo guerrillas in Laos and Combined Studies Group activities against North Vietnam. All CIA activities fell under the all-encompassing rubric 'political action,' defined as Cold-War combat, CIA style. The Special Forces White Star teams might check out of Laos to comply with international treaties; the Central Intelligence Agency did not.

The Meo guerrillas were only one of the Agency's secret mercenary armies in the region. Two others – spawned by the Chinese civil war – also operated not far from the Meo homeland. Some 12,000 veterans of Chiang Kai-shek's once-proud Kuomintang Army had been scattered over northern Burma, Thailand and Laos; they made periodic forays over the Chinese border when not trying to corner the local opium markets. The second secret army – 14,000 Khamba guerrillas – operated from inside China, in their homeland of Tibet – one of the last areas of metropolitan China to be brutally con-

quered by Mao's communists. The CIA kept these paramilitary forces going in an attempt to encourage those stubborn groups that were still resisting Mao's brand of communism.

The glue that held together the CIA's far-flung mercenary empire was Air America, the Agency's covert airline. The Khambas, the Kuomintang, the Meo – all depended on AA for food, supplies, ammunition, even economic assistance. 'Economic aid' sometimes took the form of helping with local trade problems – like bringing a tribe's opium crop to market. Some tribal chieftains either could not or would not co-operate on covert projects without such aid. At times, Agency operatives were forced to buy Meo opium harvests to save the Meo from economic ruin; reportedly, on at least one occasion raw opium was loaded into Air America planes and dumped over Communist China by a creative operative who envisioned thousands of Chinese peasants hooked on the black gooey stuff. It was

Lieutenant General William C Westmoreland, newly appointed MACV commander, and his party return to their aircraft after an inspection of Vietnamese installations at Vam Long on 1 May 1964.

107

Above: *A U-2 spy plane of the type based at Tak Le Air Force Base, Thailand, for highly classified missions.*

bussing CIA personnel (and AID, DEA and other government officials) in and out of Southeast Asia, particularly after the 1962 Geneva Accords prevented overt US Air Force resupply and transport missions into Laos. As in the early Lansdale period, AA often flew under 'humanitarian' cover to drop relief supplies to remote tribes involved in anti-communist paramilitary projects.

In the case of the Meo, AA flights truly saved them from mass starvation. As more guerrillas became involved in military operations after 1961, some 70,000 dependents of the nomadic Meo faced starvation (and displacement from their villages by vengeful communist forces). General Lansdale reportedly lobbied the Kennedy Administration for humanitarian relief. As the war's intensity increased, Air America found itself with an ever-greater number of war refugees to feed and care for.

A small number of Air America personnel participated in top secret black projects from a secret base-within-a-base at Tak Le AFB, Thailand, in the mid-1960s. The AA facility was guarded by an outer wall and moat to screen four special 'sanitized' aircraft – including U-2 and later SR-71 spy planes – and aircrews from the outside world. The planes were ostensibly US Air Force, but reportedly had screw-on and taped-on Air Force insignia, no instrument decals or serial numbers, and no tail numbers (or duplicate numbers) – allowing the aircraft to be 'laundered' for highly classified, non-attributable missions. AA crews performing these covert missions carried no identifying papers, wore no uniforms. They were treated harshly if shot down, being what they called 'status SOL' – 'S - - - Out of Luck.'

These planes and helicopters flew the most secret and dangerous missions of all – over China or the Ho Chi Minh Trail – in night drops of small 2-15 man spy teams. These teams, often dressed in Pathet Lao or NVA uniforms, sometimes spent several weeks on the ground collecting intelligence and observing infiltration routes. CIA-trained Nungs were used as trailwatchers to observe, ambush or sabotage NVA storage depots hidden in deep jungles.

After Operation SWITCHBACK and the 1962 Geneva Accords, the CIA inherited all covert operations in Laos. The Agency had set up Meo General Vang Pao's headquarters in 1961 at Long Tieng, an uninhabited mountain stronghold that soon became one of the largest Agency field headquarters in the world (second only to the Saigon station). Long Tieng grew rapidly into the second-largest city in Laos, and according to one account became 'one of the most secret spots on earth,' crammed with sophisticated electronic communication gear.

On President Kennedy's orders, the Meo took the offensive in 1963 in northern Laos, using Air America planes to ferry Meo tribesmen over the mountain peaks. In numerous lightning advances, the Meo captured Pathet Lao strongholds, quickly built up an airhead and sustained the advance's momentum. The Agency utilized the highland Meo to grab defensible mountain peaks and valleys, leaving the communists the lowlands. Meo guerrillas could then strike at will on NVA supply lines that stretched like tentacles from the North Vietnamese-Lao border down into the Mekong Delta in the South.

charged – rightly or wrongly – that Air America sometimes even *transported* opium poppies to help defray its operating costs and to keep its mercenary troops fighting. But at least no one could accuse the pragmatic airline of discrimination: AA reportedly carried both killers and doctors, wounded and dead, guns and food, opium and US agents of the Drug Enforcement Agency (seeking ways to stop foreign drug pipelines). Air America honored a contract.

Air America was the thinly disguised model for Milton Caniff's shady cartoon outfit 'Air Expendable' in the *Terry and the Pirates* comic strip. Air America operations in the Far East certainly earned it a bizarre and exotic reputation as the airline that would fly 'anything, anywhere, anytime – professionally.' AA hired its mercenary pilots – mostly ex-military pilots with a flair for adventure – as the French Foreign Legion recruited its soldiers: no questions asked if you were qualified and prepared to be shot at in performance of your mission. The company recruited the best, paid well and did not mind what you did in your spare time.

Normally, AA pay was good – $650 per month base – but the real money was to be made flying on hazardous duty or covert 'black missions' where pilots were likely to be shot at. For this type of mission, pilots might be paid promptly in envelopes stuffed with cash – no records. AA flew every conceivable type of aircraft, including multi-engine jets, ancient C-47s and DC-3s, small Cessnas, various types of helicopters and even barely airworthy 'junkers.'

AA pilots – vaguely aware of the nature of their work (but loving the excitement of it all) – spoke in simple euphemisms. The Agency was always 'the customer.' Covert missions were 'black missions,' while ammunition was 'hard rice.' Spy teams taken in were 'infils,' 'exfils' on the return trip. CIA-inspired mercenaries were always 'friendlies' and the communists 'the bad guys.' Many an AA pilot returned from a 'customer'-sponsored 'black mission' with shot-up 'exfils' and a tail peppered full of AK-47 rounds.

Commercial AA flights flew 'commuter runs,'

MACV's Studies & Observation Group

As a result of SWITCHBACK, the US Military Assistance Command, Vietnam (MACV, which replaced MAAG in 1961) inherited five 'in place' CIA agent teams in North Vietnam; the rest were either rolled up or out of contact. Even these five teams were assumed to be under communist control. MACV also assumed a large part of the CIA's covert special-operations work with the Vietnamese LLDB 'Special Branch,' redesignated the Special Exploitation Service (SES) of the Vietnamese Special Forces Command in April 1964. (In September 1967, the SES would be renamed the Strategic Technical Directorate.)

Several American special projects were formed in the next few years to perform covert operations with the SES as part of a Joint Unconventional Warfare Task Force for North Vietnam and Laos. The oldest of these special projects was MACV's Studies and Observation Group (SOG), created simultaneously with the SES in 1964. Ostensibly formed to glean lessons from the American military-advisory experience, SOG actually operated as a special operations group, conducting highly classified operations throughout Southeast Asia, directed at North Vietnamese subversive activities.

SOG was a very 'close hold' organization. Although it fell nominally under MACV cognizance, cross-border operations were outside the MACV charter, and actual supervision of SOG came from the Special Assistant for Counterinsurgency and Special Activities (SACSA) in Washington. Very few men in Washington had a 'need to know' of SOG's true mission and activities. SACSA exercised such tight control over SOG operations that details of those missions remain highly classified even today.

SOG was always commanded by a military man, although the chief was supposed to have a CIA deputy. But the Agency never filled the position, reportedly because the CIA's Southeast Asian operations chief, William Colby, objected to the set-up. The CIA had its own widespread clandestine war and apparently did not want to be subordinate to one led by a Special Forces colonel. SOG's assigned personnel eventually totaled about 2000 Americans and over 8000 indigenous personnel. All SOG personnel were volunteers, but only a special breed of unconventional warrior was accepted into SOG, whose operatives included Special Forces, Air Force Special Warfare Units, Navy SEALs, and handpicked natives, Vietnamese and assorted mercenaries – most of them airborne-qualified and with previous combat experience or Vietnam tours under their belts.

Above: *An Air America helicopter typical of those widely used in Indochina, for missions ranging from espionage to evacuation. Pilots who worked for the CIA called the agency simply 'the customer.'*

A US Navy SEAL Team dog trainer negotiates the deep grass along a Mekong Delta watercourse with his German Shepherd, which menaces the photographer to protect his handler.

SOG performed five primary missions: *Cross-border operations* to disrupt communist military activities in enemy territory; *monitoring locations of allied POWs and downed airmen* in preparation for escape and evasion (E&E) raids; *training and dispatching agents into North Vietnam* to establish resistance groups: *'black' psychological operations,* like establishing false NVA broadcasting stations in North Vietnam; and *'gray' psychological operations* in South Vietnam for radio propaganda purposes. SOG also conducted a variety of specific 'black missions,' including kidnapping, assassination and retrieval of lost documents and equipment.

SOG was divided into individual 'study groups,' each assigned to specific operational plans and focused on a distinct aspect of covert ops that traced its lineage to Lansdale's Saigon Military Mission (SMM) in 1954. A Psychological Studies Group ran such psywar activities (OPLAN/OPS 33) as beaming radio broadcasts and propaganda from secret radio transmitters professing to be in the north, and powerful 'gray' transmitters in Hué and Tay Ninh that broadcast Voice of Freedom propaganda disseminated by dissident North Vietnamese.

An Air Studies Group located in Nha Trang specialized in intelligence and aerial insertion (OPS 32) of SOG agents into 'denied areas' – those areas where overt US activities could not operate due either to hostile communist forces or to the fact that they violated international law. The Air Studies Group maintained its own dedicated air force – the

90th Special Operations Wing – composed in part of USAF UH-1F helicopters from the 20th 'Green Hornet' Squadron. It also included a C-130 transport squadron and the 219th Vietnamese Air Force H-34 helicopter squadron, which contained some of the ablest Vietnamese pilots. A SOG C-121 Constellation, crammed with sophisticated electronics gear and trailing a mile-long antenna, could overfly enemy territory and jam or black-out government frequencies and transmit SOG broadcasts.

Perhaps the most famous of the SOG observation groups was the Maritime Studies Group based in Danang. This outfit engaged in commando raids against North Vietnamese coastlines (OPLAN 34A) and in the Mekong Delta (OPS 31) with US Navy SEALs, special Vietnamese Underwater Demolition Teams (UDTs) and a private fleet of fast patrol boats. Although most SOG activities never received any publicity, '34 Alpha' operations in August 1964 are credited with triggering the famous Gulf of Tonkin incident that plunged the United States into greater military involvement in Southeast Asia.

In early August 1964, SOG PT Boats armed with 40mm automatic cannons and .50-caliber machine guns, manned by South Vietnamese crews, raided several North Vietnamese islands in an OPLAN 34A mission. In reprisal, North Vietnamese PT boats pressed at least one determined attack on nearby US Navy destroyers in the Gulf of Tonkin. The American warships, engaged in an unrelated, but still clandestine, electronic intelligence-gather-

Members of a US Navy strike team make a cautious approach to a Vietcong fortification along the Bassac River during Operation Crimson Tide.

ing mission, fired at the communist boats, while Navy jets sank or damaged several. An outraged US Congress – with little knowledge of the exact chain of events on the high seas – passed the Gulf of Tonkin resolution, which gave President Johnson *carte blanche* to escalate American involvement in the war. American air reprisals struck North Vietnam for the first time, resulting in the capture of the first American airman in the North, Navy Lt (jg) Everett Alvarez, Jr, who would endure nine years of captivity in communist prisons.

Several SOG operations were incredible, but effective. One, aimed at shutting down the North's fishing industry, involved kidnapping hundreds of North Vietnamese fishermen. After being swept from the seas, the fishermen were deposited on SOG's supersecret Phoenix Island complex off Danang. At Phoenix, Vietnamese SOG personnel treated the bewildered fishermen like vacationing tourists and told them that, for their own safety, it might be a good idea to fish only enough to provide for their own needs for awhile, as their boats might be mistaken for arms smugglers by SOG's PT boats. After several weeks of pleasureful indoctrination, the Vietnamese were stuffed with food a final time and returned to their home villages laden with gifts, including transistor radios tuned in to SOG's propaganda frequencies.

The sight of the newly returned fishermen with bulging bellies and gifts was good advertising; soon SOG was picking up willing volunteers for the royal

treatment, including 'double-dippers' eager for a second go-around. 'When the boats pulled into the canals along North Vietnam's coast,' one SOG veteran remembered, 'everybody in the village would jump into a sampan to try to get himself captured and taken off to Phoenix for a shopping trip.' But the psywar trick worked; North Vietnamese prisoners captured in the South complained of a lack of fish in their diet before their transfer.

Such SOG activities were 'plausibly deniable' – the United States would officially deny any knowledge of the action, while reaping significant psychological or military benefits. SOG operations threw the enemy off guard and demoralized the enemy population or encouraged anti-government acts at a minuscule cost in lives and resources. For other missions, like OPLAN 34A raids, SOG hired mercenaries (Asian and European) which increased the ease of deniability; reportedly, the 'mercs' also executed their missions more efficiently than the Vietnamese.

Perhaps the largest SOG operation involved the Ground Studies Group, which conducted cross-border (OPLAN 35) operations. These were a grab bag of covert missions in denied areas of Laos, Cambodia and North Vietnam: cross-border commando raids, intelligence gathering and a variety of sensitive 'black' missions.

One innovative black mission was Project ELDEST SON, involving the insertion of rigged ammunition rounds into enemy supply dumps. The rigged rounds were carefully planted in the communist supply system and set to explode upon use. The idea was to worry every Vietcong or NVA soldier about whether the next mortar round or AK-47 cartridge fired might blow up in his face. SOG psywar teams then planted rumors blaming the exploding rounds – supplied by Communist China – on Maoist inefficiency caused by the 'Great Cultural Revolution.'

SOG was restricted at first from American involvement in cross-border operations. The initial 'over-the-fence' operations, approved by President Johnson in May 1964, were code-named Leaping Lena and involved dropping all-Vietnamese six-man teams by parachute into Laos to reconnoiter the Ho Chi Minh Trail. Leaping Lena was not an overwhelming success. Many indigenous teams were quickly killed or captured (but unlike the agents in the North, the NVA did not use captured agents as propaganda, as officially the NVA was not in Laos either). Understandably, the all-Asian teams showed reluctance to jump into Laos.

However, Leaping Lena teams had demonstrated the concept of long-range reconnaissance with indigenous troops – once again. (The French had 'discovered' this over 20 years before, with their GCMA commandos.) Leaping Lena had also touched a sensitive nerve in Laos, leading to a growing need by MACV for 'strategic intelligence' on just what was coming down the Ho Chi Minh Trail. SOG began to build pressure to allow Americans over the border and to provide the indigenous teams with a steady command presence. Both the White House and the State Department strongly opposed using Americans on cross-border operations. State, in particular, was not very enthusiastic about CIA covert operations in Laos at all, which was the exception to US observance of the 1962 Geneva Accords. One early SOG commander, Colonel Donald V Blackburn (May 1964-June 1966), lobbied hard to allow Americans to participate in over-the-fence operations.

Blackburn knew the risks; he was no ordinary soldier, but a veteran special-operations type. As a young soldier in World War II, Blackburn had been trapped in the Philippines by the invading Japanese. He and several others, refusing to surrender, escaped from Bataan into the jungle to fight as guerrillas. Blackburn organized a native guerrilla force of 20,000 in five regiments, including one of Igorot headhunters (which he commanded personally). His guerrillas fought a bitter behind-the-lines struggle and continued to harass the Japanese rear after American troops returned in 1944. A 1957 movie, *Surrender, Hell!*, chronicled Blackburn's wartime experiences (he hated it, claiming it was the worst movie he had ever seen).

Blackburn ended the war as a 29-year-old full colonel and later taught his unorthodox brand of warfare at West Point. After a tour in Vietnam as an advisor, Blackburn commanded the elite 77th Special Forces Group at Fort Bragg. In this capacity, he handpicked a Lieutenant Colonel named Bull Simons to lead the White Star advisor teams into Laos in 1959. In 1964, anticipating White House approval for American-led cross-border operations, Blackburn again gave the nod to Simons, this time for the key job of chief of SOG's Ground Studies Group.

Simons, too, liked to surround himself with unconventional soldiers, men with cool heads and proven initiative under fire. He picked Special Forces Major Larry Thorne as operations officer. Thorne was a native Finn who had led his own guerrilla group against the Russians in the 1939 Russo-Finnish War. Thorne's commandos once ambushed a Russian convoy, killing 300 enemy troops without losing a single man. The highly decorated Finnish hero emigrated to the United States, joined the US Army as a private soldier and immediately volunteered for Special-Forces training. Thorne had also had a previous tour in Vietnam, as an advisor to a CIDG unit on the Cambodian border. His assistant operations officer was Major

Above: *Psychological warfare leaflets flutter from a C-47 Skytrain of the 14th Air Commando Wing.*

Left: *Leaflets urging Vietcong guerrillas to surrender safely to government forces are inserted into a special distribution chute aboard a C-47 Skytrain by USAF crewmen.*

Right: *'Skyshout' missions utilized the huge high-altitude loudspeakers shown aboard this C-47 to broadcast tape-recorded messages of warning or urges to surrender to Vietcong guerrillas in the field.*

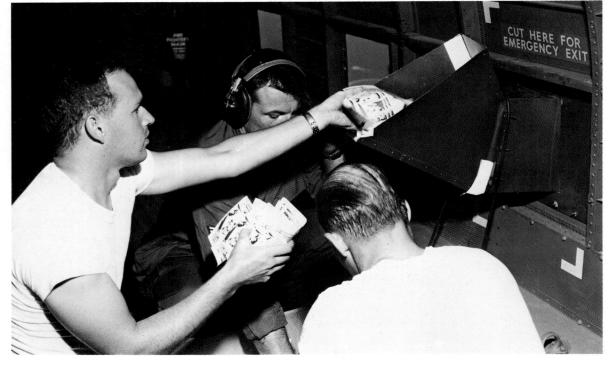

Sully Fontaine, another 'behind-the-lines' veteran. Fontaine, whose parents were French, had joined the British Army and parachuted into France in World War II as a 16-year-old to fight with *maquis* resistance groups and the OSS. He joined the US Army during the Korean War and later organized a Special Forces CIDG camp in 1963. Blackburn put Fontaine in charge of recruiting *Montagnards* for SOG missions and organizing agent networks in Cambodia and Laos. Fluent in four languages, Fontaine would sometimes conduct spy missions into Cambodia, posing as a Frenchman and rubber expert while collecting intelligence on NVA movements. Others recruited for SOG's Ground Studies Group were veteran NCOs (no rank lower than Sergeant First Class was accepted), Vietnamese members of the Special Exploitation Service (SES) and tough CIDG graduates. All Group members trained at the Vietnamese LLDB camp at Long Than, a secret facility outside Saigon.

American-led cross-border operations in Laos were finally approved in July 1965, after considerable pressure from Blackburn, General William Westmoreland, the JCS and CINCPAC (Commander-In-Chief-Pacific) Admiral Grant Sharp. SOG had accumulated a list of 500 potential ground targets, based on aerial reconnaissance photos which it was to verify on its initial mission – code-named Shining Brass.

Once the project was approved, Blackburn prepared a three-phase program: (1) Reconnaissance to verify local trails and supply depots; (2) Insertion of commando units to exploit targets, supported by airpower; and (3) Organizing local indigenous forces into resistance groups to harass the Ho Chi Minh Trail – as CIA-backed guerrillas were trying to do from bases on the Plain of Jars in Laos. This final task envisioned the classic Special Forces mission, which in turn conformed to the old French GCMA *modus operandi*.

State Department placed some restrictions on the first mission, limiting SOG's recon teams to penetrations of no more than 20 kms inside Laos. The first Shining Brass mission was launched from the Kham Duc Special Forces camp on 18 October 1965. The recon team consisted of two US Special Forces sergeants and four Vietnamese on a five-day mission to reconnoiter a suspected truck terminal 15 'klicks' (kilometers) into Laos. Poor weather delayed the launch, but eventually the team's chopper and a gunship carrying Major Thorne lifted off for the drop.

On the third day of careful penetration, crossing many fresh trails used by enemy patrols, the team located the truck park; using hand signals to communicate, they worked slowly toward the sound of heavy trucks – incongruous in the deep jungle. Not far from the park, automatic-weapons fire – probably Soviet-made AK-47 – felled the Vietnamese point man, springing a communist ambush.

The SOG team beat a hasty retreat and quickly lost the communist patrol, then called for a rapid extraction to safety after marking the location. US Air Force F-105 fighter-bombers based in Udorn, Thailand, did the rest, striking the supply base with 88 sorties. The many secondary explosions indicated that SOG had fingered a major ammo depot for a bull's eye. The mission's success was marred only

by the loss of Larry Thorne, whose escort chopper disappeared in the swirling fog during the infiltration drop. No trace of Thorne, his chopper or his crew was ever found.

Subsequent helicopter insertions for Shining Brass missions would customarily take off at first light or at dusk. Although the enemy heard the noisy machines' approach, drop ships would touch down several times to disguise the true point of insertion. 'After you land,' Blackburn taught his men, 'just get lost in the jungle and wait. Make them hunt for you. When you hear them, you can do the ambushing.'

The recon teams' chief mission was to reconnoiter, using silent patrol techniques; traveling light, stealth and camouflage played a large part in performing this mission. Most SOG teams abandoned the standard-issue camouflage jungle suits, as they were a dead giveaway for a moving soldier; SOG veterans preferred black suits – much like those worn by VC and NVA guerrillas. SOG troops also carried 'sterile' non-US issue weapons like the Swedish 'K' 9mm submachine gun, the French MAT 49 submachine gun, or the Soviet-made AK-47 assault rifle. Recon teams also left behind identification papers; as all operations were 'deniable,' capture meant treatment as spies and certain death. Blackburn gave his men maps deliberately altered by 10 kilometers; in case of capture, this could confuse the enemy as to the accuracy of his own maps. For long-range patrols that lasted nearly a week, SOG issued a special ration – called Patrol Indigenous Ration (PIR) – consisting of individual plastic bags of instant rice with fish or meat that became a meal with the addition of water.

Simons' recon teams made a total of seven crossings into Laos in 1965, all successful in terms of target verification and valuable intelligence brought back. In one of those missions, team leader Master Sergeant Richard Meadows discovered a surprising cache hidden in the jungle: a full battery of Soviet-made howitzers – still coated with thick Cosmoline

preservative. Meadows removed a firing mechanism and hand-delivered it to an ecstatic General Westmoreland. Meadows' find was the first hard evidence of heavy Soviet war matériel making its way down the Ho Chi Minh Trail – and a signal of Hanoi's intentions to continue escalating the ground war in South Vietnam. For this prize, Sergeant Meadows received from Westmoreland one of only two battlefield commissions handed out during 'Westy's' tenure at MACV.

Westmoreland was well satisfied with the fruits of SOG's strategic reconnaissance. However, until the arrival of major American (conventional) combat units in 1966, SOG's Shining Brass operations were conditioned by policy considerations stemming from the 1962 Geneva Conference that 'neutralized' Laos. Even recon-team-directed airstrikes required the permission (on a target-by-target basis) of the US Ambassador in Vientiane, Laos. Many unconventional soldiers – aware of the major truck parks, supply depots and extensive NVA trail-defense systems – chafed under these restrictions. Eventually, some of them were relaxed. The 20-km limit and the laborious airstrike procedures were retained, but others – such as prohibitions on helicopter insertion – were dropped as impractical in the rugged mountain terrain.

Blackburn's tenure at SOG also coincided with the buildup of American troops in South Vietnam (from 24,000 advisors in early 1965 to over 200,000 a year later). This event stole much of the limelight from what had been a previously low-key conflict of nominal American 'advisors' and highly classified covert missions. But to the men of SOG's Shining Brass operations, the enemy too was engaged in a comparable buildup – on the Ho Chi Minh Trail – that received far less publicity than the American version. By the end of 1965, battalions and regiments of hard-core NVA regulars – no longer 're-groupees' – surged down the Ho Chi Minh Trail by the thousands.

Above: *A 17-year-old Kit Carson Scout (left), who had joined the Vietcong at the age of 14, helps question an equally youthful suspect.*

Opposite: *Suspects apprehended in an Operation Market Time foray in the South China Sea are transported from their junk to USS* Forster, *which will deliver them to South Vietnamese authorities at the seaside city of Vung Tao.*

The Men in Black
Pajamas: 1960-68

On 19 May 1959, the date of Ho Chi Minh's 69th birthday, Brigadier General Vo Bam was summoned to the Office of the Party Central Military Committee in Hanoi to accept a special secret assignment. A few months earlier, the party had decided to escalate the struggle in the South, moving from a strategy of political subversion to one of armed insurrection against the Diem regime. As part of this new strategy, Bam was entrusted with the task of opening a supply route to the revolution in the South. 'This line will be a special trail on which cadres, combatants, arms and medical supplies will be sent to the South,' he was told.

Doan 559: Building the Rear Base

Later on the afternoon of 19 May, Bam spoke with Tran Luong, who had been entrusted with rebuilding and organizing Liberation forces in the South. Diem's war against the religious sects, the persecution of former Vietminh who had remained after the partition and the infiltration of local party cells by the secret police had decimated their ranks. By 1959, party membership in the South had shrunk to 5000. Actual armed forces – from the party's secret units of former Vietminh, sect remnants and highland minority dissidents – numbered only 2000. Another 3000 guerrillas were also available, but they had little or no combat training or experience.

Luong told Bam that the party political bureau had instructed him to send 500 cadres and 7000 weapons to the South in order to organize 700 self-defense platoons. The cadres would all be southern regroupees. Great care was to be taken to hide Hanoi's expanded role so as to give the impression of adherence to the Geneva Accords and to maintain the illusion that the insurrection in South Vietnam was an internal revolution against a repressive regime. 'This route must be kept absolutely secret,' cautioned Luong. 'It must not be allowed to become a beaten path, that is, not a single footprint, cigarette butt, or broken twig, may be left on it after the men's passage.'

Bam was assigned 500 men for the task, whom he organized into a transportation unit named *Doan 559*, the numerical equivalent for May 1959, the date of the plan's inception. The men were chosen from the 305th Division, regroupees who had fought in the southern Central Highlands during the war with the French. To hide their true identity, they were issued 'pajama-like costumes and plaited-leaf helmets,' reported Bam. Armed with captured French weapons, they outfitted themselves with rucksacks, canteens and other captured or abandoned French military gear purchased at local flea markets.

After scouting possible base camps, Bam selected Khe Ho, a small village in the far western reaches of Vinh Linh Province just above the Demarcation Line, as the jumping-off point for his units. Follow-

Previous pages: A Special Forces team member on the watch.

Opposite: An impassive Vietcong is surprised in his bunker by enemy lights.

Below: On the right, an NVA soldier with a Soviet-made SKS rifle, wearing captured US Army jungle boots. The Vietcong soldier at left wears the customary black pajamas and a woven bamboo hat covered with black plastic; he carries a Communist-Chinese supplied AK-47 rifle.

ing lumberjack trails and secret paths used by the brigade guarding the Demarcation Line, Battalion 301, the first of the transportation units to be organized, took up positions at Khe Ho early in June. The battalion was divided into 12 platoons. Two platoons remained at Khe Ho, while three more were assigned to man three way-stations between the main base and the Ben Hai River, which ran through the center of the Demilitarized Zone (DMZ). The seven remaining platoons would man seven camps dotting the way from there to Phin, a village south of Highway 9 in Quang Tri Province, where they would deliver the supplies to southern liberation forces. From there, they would be transported by local units farther south along 'Reunification Trail,' a system of crude jungle paths organized a few years before as a line of communication linking guerrilla forces in the northern provinces with those in the highlands.

On 10 June the seven platoons crossed the Ben Hai River to deliver the first batch of supplies and man their stations in South Vietnam. Although the route chosen wound through the sparsely populated terrain of mountainous jungle that made up the eastern foothills of the Truong Son mountain range along the Laotian border, South Vietnamese Government troops had established a number of outposts in the area along Highway 9. This strategic road, which ran westward from the port of Cua Viet through to Khe Sanh and into lower Laos, was the Saigon Government's first line of defense south of the DMZ. On 20 August, Bam finally received word from the commander of Battalion 301: 'All goods delivered safely.' *Doan 559* had successfully penetrated the barrier between North and South.

Bam began making arrangements immediately to send teams of cadres along the secret route. In January 1960, a training base for infiltrators was established at Son Tay, a town on the Red River northwest of Hanoi. There the 324th Division, com-

Top right: *Members of a North Vietnamese Volunteers Brigade in a jungle classroom, where a spent rocket serves as an impromptu blackboard.*
Right: *A Vietcong propaganda message scrawled on the wall of Outpost Ly Van Manh. It reads in part: 'The Americans will be crushed and Diem will be crushed, exposing the US culprits.'*
Opposite: *US Navy SEALs offload captured Vietcong equipment after a successful raid on enemy base camps along the Bassac River.*

121

prised mainly of regroupees, underwent special training prior to their journey south. *Doan 559* was also expanded to include the newly formed Battalion 603, a 107-man unit organized to supervise infiltration and supply by sea. But until enough boats could be built and safe sea routes found, the majority of infiltration was by land.

Battalion 301 was reinforced to a strength of 440 men and equipped with a few trucks, 30 horses and three elephants to help transport supplies. Since there were few existing roads or trails, however, the bulk of the supplies was carried by hand. Porters toting bundles of four rifles or 20-kilo cases of ammunition on their shoulders worked their way across the mountainous jungle terrain day after day, month after month. Wearing little more than a pair of shorts, a patched shirt and a leaf hat, they lived on balls of rice and salt during the grueling trek south. Carefully avoiding enemy patrols, they scrupulously adhered to the instruction: 'No footprint, no cooking smoke, no sound of conversation.'

By the end of 1960, US and South Vietnamese intelligence analysts estimated that more than 4500 communist soldiers had infiltrated into the South along with untold quantities of arms, ammunition and other supplies. In response, the South Vietnamese began establishing more outposts in the mountainous border regions and attempted to subvert infiltration activities through the use of spies and commando teams. Finding more frequent obstacles in their path along the eastern edges of the Truong Son, Party General Secretary Le Duan asked Bam to find an alternative route that would attract less enemy attention. Bam suggested using the western side of the mountain range in Lao territory.

A right-wing coup in Vientiane in December 1960, which led to the resumption of civil war in Laos, proved the perfect vehicle for the North Vietnamese to secure the territory in the Laotian panhandle through which they could expand their infiltration network. Under the pretext of supporting the Pathet Lao in their fight with the rightists, NVA regulars pushed the Royal Laotian Army out of the highlands in the spring of 1961 and secured an area 80 kilometers wide from Tchepone to Muong Phin. In return for helping to consolidate Pathet-Lao liberated areas into a secure base area for continued guerrilla operations, the NVA obtained unimpeded use of the Lao panhandle adjacent to the Vietnamese border.

Utilizing existing roads and trails and blazing new ones through the forests and jungle, the North Vietnamese gradually began developing a network of communication and supply lines that stretched its tentacles across the entire eastern section of southern Laos and into northeastern Cambodia. The infiltration network, which came to be known as the Ho Chi Minh Trail, had doubled its capacity by the end of 1961, and, according to one North Vietnamese source, was able 'to organize the march of 10,000 reinforcements to various battlefields.' US intelligence sources confirmed the boast, estimating that the number of troops infiltrated down the trail had more than doubled, from 6295 in 1961 to 12,857 in 1962. *Doan 559*, which had expanded to 5000 men plus an engineering regiment by 1963, enlarged the infiltration system to include some 1000 kilometers

US B-57 jet bombers destroyed in the Vietcong shelling of Bien Hoa Airbase, where an estimated 100 rounds of 81mm mortar wiped out or disabled 28 US warplanes (November 1964).

The 11th Armored Cavalry Regiment on the move in Operation Junction City, south of Tay Ninh, in February 1967. Junction City was the first major overt operation of the US involvement phase.

of roads and trails. By 1964 an estimated 30-35,000 regroupees, over a third of the total that had gone North in 1954, had returned to the South.

Most of the infiltrators had seen combat either in the war with the French or in Laos. They received specialized training at one of a number of camps near Hanoi, where they were instructed in communications, demolitions, command and staff, and other technical skills. Others were skilled organizers, specially trained to help recruit and mold new armed units. They would form the core of new Vietcong units in the South, pulling in experienced guerrillas from local and regional companies and new recruits whom they would organize and train into new, combat-ready battalions, regiments, divisions and support units.

Buoyed by the growing flow of arms and supplies, and bolstered by the arrival of increasing numbers of regroupees from the North, the Vietcong grew in strength and confidence. Their ranks swelled to an estimated 17,000 armed regulars by late 1961; by 1964, the number had doubled to 34,000 men. Guerrilla forces increased from 3000 men in 1960 to some 72,000 in 1964.

The Vietcong concentrated mainly in former Vietminh strongholds, specifically in the eastern edges of the Central Highlands, along the Cambodian border, in the heavily forested areas north of Saigon and in the southern tip of the Mekong Delta. They took advantage of the natural terrain in these areas – impenetrable forests, inaccessible mountains, thick jungle and vast river deltas interspersed with hundreds of waterways, canals and rice fields – all ideally suited to guerrilla warfare.

Employing hit-and-run tactics, the Vietcong ambushed government patrols and convoys and overran isolated outposts. The number of VC attacks on government outposts and villages nearly tripled in 1961. They also engaged in terrorist attacks designed to weaken the government's control in the countryside. Between 1959 and 1961, the number of local South Vietnamese officials assassinated rose from 1200 to 4000 per year. On 18 September a guerrilla force seized the city of Phuoc

Vinh, capital of Phuoc Long Province, publicly beheaded the province chief and withdrew before an ARVN rescue force arrived. Combining the iron fist of selective terrorism and the velvet glove of propaganda, which offered promises of land reform and a better life, the Vietcong slowly expanded their influence in the countryside.

The deteriorating situation spurred a substantial increase in American support for the Diem regime. By December 1962, US military personnel in the South numbered over 11,300, more than three times the number at the beginning of the year. The South Vietnamese Army (ARVN) was enlarged to 220,000 men armed with small arms and machine guns, heavy artillery, communications equipment, transport aircraft, armored personnel carriers (APCs) and other military hardware provided by the Americans. In addition to advisory and logistical assistance, the Americans also provided helicopters for rapid deployment and fighter-bombers for air cover of ARVN troops, creating a highly mobile and heavily armed Regular ARVN.

Throughout 1962, ARVN units equipped with APCs, transported and supported by US helicopters, gradually began slicing their way through what historian Bernard Fall labeled the 'arc of insurgency' that had been tightening around Saigon. At the urging of their US advisors, ARVN units abandoned their garrison mentality and launched large-scale operations against guerrilla strongholds that had long been considered invulnerable. ARVN's new-found mobility, the extension of government control into areas previously under undisputed communist control, and the continued influx of US equipment and advisors all created serious problems for the Vietcong.

However, ARVN's new-found confidence was shattered on 2 January 1963, when elements of the ARVN 7th Division and local Civil Guard battalions attempted to trap a smaller Vietcong force near the hamlet of Ap Bac west of Saigon. Despite the carefully laid plans and the use of US helicopters, the South Vietnamese were soundly beaten. Some 200 regulars of the Vietcong 514th Battalion, reinforced

by local guerrillas and armed with nothing more powerful than three machine guns and a dozen Browning automatic rifles, took less than a dozen casualties while inflicting 168 casualties on an ARVN force of 2000 men backed by artillery, APCs and fighter-bombers. The Lao Dong Party history claimed that Ap Bac 'proved that the South Vietnamese Army [the Vietcong] and the people were completely capable of *militarily* defeating the United States in the "special war."'

Vietcong successes against US-backed ARVN forces on the battlefield were accompanied by increasing domestic unrest within South Vietnam. Buddhist and student demonstrations against the Diem regime that summer, ruthlessly suppressed by government security forces, triggered a political crisis that ultimately led to the overthrow of Diem by a group of rebellious generals in November, as described. The resulting political chaos severely hampered the war effort.

During a 10-day conference in December 1963, North Vietnamese Communist Party leaders resolved that it was 'time for the North to...bring into fuller play its role as the revolutionary base for the whole nation.' Shipments of arms, including modern Russian- and Chinese-made weapons, were increased, as were the number of troops sent to the South. But the pool of available regroupees of military age had run dry. It was now necessary to begin sending Northern-born NVA regulars to bolster Southern liberation forces.

The first regular NVA unit to infiltrate the South was the 808th Battalion, which left soon after the Gulf of Tonkin incident in August 1964. The 95th Regiment arrived in December, and seven more would be sent in 1965. By the spring of 1966, a total of 14 NVA regiments, or approximately 20,000 men, were operating in the South. These regular NVA units remained as independent forces rather than being integrated into local Southern forces. Their presence in the South was masked by an elaborate ruse designed to deceive US intelligence. Each regiment was divided in half and each half then reinforced to full strength. One was sent South while the other remained in the North, so that there would be no noticeable change in Hanoi's order of battle.

In December 1964, the communists scored a major triumph during a month-long battle between 3000 ARVN troops and 1500 Vietcong, including the newly formed 9th Division, near the town of Binh Gia. Although the 9th Division was the first to receive the more modern weapons, including Russian AK-47 assault rifles, Chinese 7.62mm machine guns, RPG-2 rocket launchers and 82mm mortars, they were still outclassed by ARVN's superiority in heavy weapons, air support and helicopters. But by employing surprise attacks, rapid withdrawals and feints, the VC divided and ambushed ARVN forces, inflicting heavy casualties in the process.

To Hanoi, Binh Gia marked a pivotal point in the course of the rebellion. It indicated clearly the bankruptcy of America's 'special war' strategy by proving that communist units, with support and training from the North and some upgrading of their weaponry, could defeat larger, heavily armed, US-backed heliborne ARVN units. Hanoi's leaders believed that, through the combination of political chaos and VC successes on the battlefield, they were on the verge of realizing their goal of 'reunification.' But it was clear that Vietcong forces in the South were still not strong enough to seize the opportunity without active outside support.

Party leaders realized expanded support for the struggle in the South would probably result in deeper American involvement. They predicted an abandonment of the special-war strategy by the Americans in favor of a 'limited war' and the eventual introduction of US combat troops. Unable to hope to match America's superior firepower, mobility and technology, Hanoi would shift to a strategy of protracted war, in which its forces would be geared to denying the Americans victory. Inspired by Mao's doctrine of revolutionary warfare, which stressed the importance of the force of will, communist troops were told that discipline, enthusiasm and willingness to face hardships would help them prevail against America's unlimited and technically superior military resources. Their ultimate objective was to undermine the Americans' strategy for success and to keep them on the defensive long enough to convince them of the futility of their effort; eventually, they would withdraw of their own accord.

The North would continue to provide its southern comrades with logistical and operational support, but without committing the major part of its own forces, which were essential to the ultimate success of its protracted-war strategy. North Vietnam would become the 'Great Rear Base' area – a sanctuary and source of supply for the war in the South.

Traveling Down the Ho Chi Minh Trail

North Vietnam's primary lifeline to the battle in the South was the Ho Chi Minh Trail, the ever-expanding spider web of roads, trails and mountain paths that wound its way southward through the Laotian panhandle. At the head of this web were the few rudimentary 'highways' running through the mountain passes that bisected the rugged Truong Son range at Mu Gia, Ban Karai and Ban Raving. The supply columns then turned onto smaller roads

and tracks that coursed their way through the eastern ridges of the Truong Son mountains. Running alongside these roads was a complicated network of well-concealed trails, hacked out of the jungle by hand, used by NVA troops during their march from North to South Vietnam.

By the end of the war, the trail would include more than 13,000 kilometers of roads and trails, creating a vast military supply corridor 50 miles wide at some points. It was a redundant system of double and triple bypasses and footpaths, real and phony truck depots and base areas, among which traffic constantly shifted to confuse American reconnaissance efforts and to protect against commando raids or airstrikes. Hanoi went to great lengths to keep its infiltration routes hidden from the international community, as well as from the Americans, even going so far as to disavow the existence of North Vietnamese soldiers captured by government forces in Laos.

The dense bamboo and brushwood forests and triple-canopy jungle that blanketed the Truong Son range provided excellent cover for the infiltration system. The North Vietnamese used the rugged terrain to their advantage, often clearing new roads, then replacing the jungle cover atop the road, making it invisible from the air. Floating bridges, made of small boats and bamboo roadways, which could be cut loose and tied to the riverbank by day to hide them from observation aircraft, were used to cross streams and rivers.

Thousands of North Vietnamese and Laotian soldiers and workers manned the network of communications and support facilities necessary to maintain and defend the trail system. By the late 1960s, some 40-50,000 civilian laborers (*dan cong*) worked along the trail, building new roads, repairing others and transporting supplies. Among them were groups of young (some of them teen-age) volunteers, mainly girls and women between the ages of 15 and 30. Organized into 'Youth Shock Brigades,' they were provided with clothing, room and board and five *dong* ($1.50) a month and lived in temporary shelters along the trail. Not all the workers on the trail were such enthusiastic volunteers. The North Vietnamese also conscripted local tribesmen and employed prisoners as forced laborers.

The youth gangs, porters and forced laborers all worked under the supervision of *Doan 559*, which itself had grown to include some 30-50,000 troops. These forces were assigned to one of the major base camps, known as *Binh Tram*, 11 of which had been identified in Laos by 1970. Essentially logistical headquarters for a particular area of operation, each *Binh Tram* was assigned a transportation, signal and engineer battalion, as well as an infantry and one or more artillery battalions. These units were responsible for moving men and supplies through their zone of control, and maintaining and defending their portion of the trail system.

Away from these heavily guarded base areas were a number of *Commo-Liaison* stations. Scattered about a day's march apart, these way stations were located off narrow paths and buried deep in the jungle to avoid detection. They were staffed by 15 to 20 men who provided infiltrators with food, shelter, medical aid and guidance to the next station. Once

Above: *Two members of the Fifth Marines display a warning sign posted in the jungle by Vietcong.*
Right: *The US Marines were among the first US troops involved in training and pacification efforts, notably in the Demilitarized Zone, or DMZ.*

troops and supplies reached one of the base areas at the end of the trail along the border, *Doan 559*'s responsibility ended. The soldiers were assigned to local combat forces, while the supplies were moved into the interior by local transport squads.

As the war escalated and infiltration routes expanded, trucks began replacing porters and bicycles in the transportation role. By 1965, 51 percent of the supplies sent South went via mechanized means. Infiltrating soldiers, however, continued to make the journey on foot, occasionally hitching a short truck ride if they were lucky. The journey began at one of the many infiltration staging areas in the southern panhandle of North Vietnam, where the men received new clothing and equipment and were issued forged documents to conceal their identity. Troops traveling from Vinh in Nghe An Province,

one of the main infiltration staging areas in North Vietnam, took an average of two months to reach the South Vietnamese border – three if they made the 600-mile trek to the southernmost way station on the trail. Although the trek was less grueling than it had been in the early 1960s due to expansion of the trail and the work of *Doan 599*, it was still an extremely hazardous journey.

During the southwest monsoon, from May to September, the trail was constantly blanketed with a layer of thick rain clouds. The incessant heavy rains transformed dirt roads and trails into muddy, slippery tracks, and turned streams into raging torrents that slowed foot traffic considerably and brought motorized transport to a virtual standstill.

Tran Mai Nam, an NVA war correspondent, recalled his journey along the Ho Chi Minh Trail in

By 1965, half the supplies reaching South Vietnam from 'the Great Rear Base' in the North were transported by trucks, rather than porters or cyclists, as in the 1950s and early 1960s.

ARVN soldiers make an impressive appearance in National Day ceremonies attended by civil and military leaders in Saigon: 1 November 1964.

A Vietcong camp in the Mekong Delta is hit by automatic-weapon and rocket fire from US Navy UH-1B Iroquois helicopters.

mid-1966 as a 'torturous' trek through 'impenetrable jungle' along paths that seemed 'to liquify under our feet.' In spots, segments of the trail had been washed away by the torrential rains. 'The packs on our shoulders seem to have doubled their weight.... You feel penetrated by the water,' he wrote, 'and you have the intolerable impression that mushrooms are about to grow on your clothes and even on your skin.' The heavy, incessant rains also increased a soldier's susceptibility to mosquitoes and disease. Approximately 15 percent of the troops moving down the trail succumbed to illnesses, mainly malaria.

While the monsoon rains made life miserable for the North Vietnamese, periods of good weather, especially during the October to April dry season, brought another, more deadly threat – American reconnaissance aircraft and fighter-bombers.

In the spring of 1964, carrier-based US Navy photo reconnaissance jets began regular overflights of Laos. When these 'Yankee Team' flights confirmed reports of the increased levels of NVA infiltration, Washington authorized secret bombing missions against the Ho Chi Minh Trail as part of its covert pressure program against North Vietnam. The Americans, as anxious as Hanoi to avoid the appearance of violating the Geneva neutrality agreement on Laos, at first employed the US-backed Royal Laotian Air Force for the task. Washington delivered more than two dozen T-28 Nomad fighter-bombers to the RLAF and sent a special team of Air Force air commandos to help train Laotian pilots in the new planes. The Americans also contracted a number of Thai mercenaries to fly unmarked T-28s on raids against the trail.

But these surrogate air forces achieved little success, barely denting the trail network. In December, President Johnson authorized Operation Barrel Roll – limited air strikes by USAF jets based in Thailand and Navy carrier-based aircraft. Two strikes per week, consisting of no more than four aircraft each, were targeted against the northernmost reaches of the trail. Air activity in Laos increased dramatically in March 1965, after initiation of full-scale bombing operations against North Vietnam. While Operation Barrel Roll continued to hit targets in northeastern Laos, a new campaign, code-named Steel Tiger, was initiated against infiltration routes in the eastern edges of the southern panhandle. Yet a third campaign was created later in the year, when the Steel-Tiger area of operations was divided in two. Steel Tiger continued in the section of the panhandle north of the 17th parallel, while bombing operations farther south, adjacent to the South Vietnamese border, now became known as Tiger Hound. By 1966 US planes were flying more than 1000 sorties per month in Laos and the numbers kept increasing. Between 1964 and 1970, the US would drop more than 2.2 million tons of bombs onto infiltration routes in Laos. Despite the intensity of effort, the air campaign remained shrouded in secrecy.

According to Colonel Robert Tyrell, the US Air Force attaché assigned to the US Embassy in Vientiane, American military involvement in Laos was kept 'in the black.' When Tyrell's office, which was legally limited to less than a dozen officers and men by the terms of the 1962 neutralization pact, became unable to cope with the rising level of air operations, Washington sent an additional 117 military advisors under civilian cover into Laos in 1966 in what was code-named Project 404. Nearly half were Air Force personnel, primarily intelligence and communications specialists who worked in the secret air-operations center in Vientiane, or in the embassy itself. They wore civilian clothes, carried IDs identifying them as employees of a variety of civilian government agencies, and were threatened with court-martial if they were caught talking to newsmen.

Since no formal US military command structure existed in Laos, bombing operations were controlled by the US ambassador, William Sullivan, through the Air Attaché Office. Targeting requests submitted by the Air Force, Army, CIA and Laotian authorities were reviewed and approved by Project 404 personnel in accordance with a series of guidelines set down by the Ambassador, who had the unenviable task of trying to satisfy all these conflicting demands while keeping the lid on the bombing level to preserve the image of American neutrality. Just as the North Vietnamese denied the existence of the trail, the Americans denied they were bombing it.

Main picture: *As North Vietnam's air defenses improved, US A-1Es were restricted to missions over South Vietnam.*
Inset: *An F-105G armed with a Shrike missile over Laos.*

The North Vietnamese moved the majority of their supplies at night to lessen their chances of being detected from the air. Truck drivers began their journey at dusk, groping their way over narrow, winding roads in the darkness. Their headlights turned off, they were guided by white stakes interspersed along the roadside and teen-age volunteers who acted as 'traffic cops' at key intersections. At dawn, they pulled into one of over a thousand camouflaged truck parks scattered along the trail.

The Air Force countered with infrared cameras, side- and downward-looking radar, and low-level-light detection devices, including the Starlight Scope, which could magnify existing star- and moonlight up to 50,00 times. Smaller versions of the scope could be held by observers in low-flying reconnaissance planes, while larger versions were fitted into the bellies of C-123 transports, which also carried flares to illuminate targets once they were located.

Valuable intelligence also came from Mao guerrillas and ethnic Chinese Nung hill tribesmen, recruited by the CIA to act as trail watchers. Infiltrating behind enemy lines, they radioed information on truck and troop movements to aircraft overhead. Some of the tribesmen who knew no English were given special radio transmitters consisting of a series of buttons labeled by a picture of a truck, a platoon of soldiers, a tank and so forth. Each time he saw one of these objects pass, the trail watcher pushed the appropriate button, which sent a coded signal to listening operatives.

The North Vietnamese employed their own teams of spotters who scanned the skies above the trail, ready to sound the warning alert once they heard or saw American planes approaching. Warning signals varied from crude gongs to a sentry's rifle shot, and even a sophisticated system of flashing lights which indicated the plane's line of approach so that trucks could take appropriate evasive action.

By day, the Americans bombed key 'choke points,' intersections along heavily traveled roads and narrow mountain passes, in hope of slowing down traffic and creating impassable bottlenecks. They also dropped delayed-action bombs, mines that buried themselves in the ground, and tiny anti-personnel 'Gravel' mines – explosives-filled cloth packets that could blow off a man's foot.

The North Vietnamese countered the Americans' choke-point bombing tactics by simply rerouting traffic along one of the many bypasses that had been cut out of the jungle while laborers converged on the scene, repairing the damage, clearing rubble, filling in bomb craters and removing or defusing mines. The enemy 'never runs out of roads,' commented one Air Force spokesman. 'It just drives you nuts.'

Bombing operations also became more hazardous as the number of anti-aircraft batteries defending the trail gradually increased in number. By 1967 the North Vietnamese had deployed more than 10,000 AA artillery pieces within Laos. The introduction of larger caliber, long-range, radar-directed weapons exposed US planes to greater hazards. Slower, propeller-driven planes were particularly vulnerable and had to be replaced by faster jet fighter-bombers, which flew at higher altitudes and were not as accurate.

The Americans were constantly searching for ways to improve anti-infiltration efforts along the trail. A number of schemes were proposed, including some rather bizarre ones. Helicopters, rigged up with sirens, flashing lights and loudspeakers, were sent over the trail at night in an effort to scare superstitious North Vietnamese truck drivers. Another suggestion surfaced: training pigeons to home in on trucks. Once the bird landed, a metal detector attached to its foot would trigger an explosive charge strapped to its back and blow up the truck. There was only one drawback, however. No one could figure out how to teach the pigeons to distinguish a communist truck from a non-communist one.

Other, more scientific, schemes were also devised, including an ultra-secret weather modification program conducted jointly by the Defense Department and the CIA. Begun in July 1967, and

Opposite: *US Air Force F-100 Super Sabers strike Vietcong targets in the South in 1967.*
Above: *This poignant picture of a US pilot captured in 1967 was used on a North Vietnamese-issued stamp for propaganda purposes.*

A US Air Force B-52 Stratofortress drops bombs over a suspected Vietcong stronghold in 1966. Excessive reliance on 'big-gun' American air support may have inhibited the growth of a truly autonomous South Vietnamese military machine capable of standing up against communist pressure.

known by the successive code-names Compatriot, Intermediary and Popeye, it was designed to increase normal monsoon-season rainfall by seeding clouds with silver and lead iodide in an effort to turn dirt roads and trails into muddy bogs, create landslides, wash out river crossings and swell the many streams that the North Vietnamese used to transport supplies by raft and sampan into raging torrents. An even more highly classified part of the program, supervised by the CIA, dumped tons of specially developed chemicals onto the trails which reacted with the rain to turn the hard-packed dirt into an impassable goo. The Air Force also expanded its 'Ranch Hand' chemical defoliation program into Laos in an attempt to strip the trail of its natural cover.

But the biggest anti-infiltration project to evolve from US technology was 'Igloo White,' an offshoot of Secretary of Defense McNamara's 'electronic-fence' concept. The original proposal envisioned a barrier of barbed wire and electronic sensors stretching across the DMZ through Laos to the Thai border. Although the idea was eventually scrapped as too costly and impractical, the Defense Department decided to use the sensors that had been developed and tested to replace the clandestine trail watchers employed in Laos.

Under the aegis of the top-secret Defense Communications Planning Group, a collection of civilian scientists and military men organized to develop, test and implement the sensor program. Operation Igloo White was put into operation in November 1967. A special command, known as Task Force Alpha, was created within the 7th Air Force to install, maintain and monitor the project. Employing a variety of military and even Air America aircraft, Task Force Alpha began 'seeding' the sensors along infiltration routes.

The sensors came in a variety of types and shapes. The Spikebuoy was a 5½-foot-long cylindrical device that buried itself in the ground on impact, leaving only a small plastic antenna disguised as a bush or weed above ground. The Acoubuoy, similarly shaped but only three feet long, was dropped by parachute to snag itself in the tops of trees or triple-canopy jungle. Both were acoustic sensors that detected and transmitted sounds nearby. The most widely used sensor was the Adsid, which resembled a thin mortar shell. Like the Spikebuoy, it buried itself in the ground, leaving only its plant-like antennae visible. The Adsid registered nearby ground vibrations, created by a passing truck or a column of troops, which activated its battery-operated transmitter. A fourth type, the Acousid, combined an acoustic and vibration-sensitive capability.

All four types of sensors could activate themselves or be triggered by remote control from a Lockheed EC-121R jammed with radio and electronic equipment. Technicians aboard these aircraft constantly monitored the sensors and relayed the signals to Task Force Alpha's Infiltration Surveillance Center at Nakhon Phanom, just across the border in Thailand. An enormous concrete structure in the middle of the jungle, the center was staffed by Air Force and civilian technicians who collected the information and fed the data into two IBM-360-65 computers, which collated, analyzed and inter-

preted the signals coming in from a variety of sensor fields. In some instances, the information would trigger an immediate air strike by US fighter-bomber jets held constantly on alert in what was known as Operation Commando Bolt. But the sensors also gave American air commanders the ability to monitor traffic patterns on the trail to determine concentrations of troops, truck parks and natural choke points which could be targeted for air strikes. 'We wired the Ho Chi Minh Trail like a drugstore pinball machine and we plugged it in every night,' said one Air Force officer.

The sensor system helped to increase the effectiveness of US bombing efforts. By 1970, Air Force officials claimed that only one ton in every 32 shipped down the trail made it to the battlefield in the South. But according to Pentagon estimates, this was still too much. Only 60 tons of supplies a month were needed to sustain the fighting capability of communist forces in the South, and more than that was still slipping through. Bombing could place a ceiling on the level of infiltration, but it could not close down the trail.

Hazardous duties in the secret war included exploration of mined and booby-trapped underground complexes, as in this 1965 search-and-destroy mission.

Sanctuaries and Combat Villages

Following the trail to the opposite end of the supply pipeline, an NVA soldier found himself in one of a dozen or more base camps in Laos or Cambodia astride the South Vietnamese border, which acted as rear-supply and staging areas for launching attacks in the South. Located across the border in neutral territory, they provided the communists with a virtual sanctuary from regular American troops who were prohibited from following. While camps in Laos were subjected to US bombing attacks, those in Cambodia were immune from air attack until 1969, when President Nixon secretly ordered B-52 strikes against them. Until then, they only had to worry about occasional forays by SOG sabotage and intelligence-gathering teams.

The scope and breadth of these base camps was startling. 'There were hard-surface roads [and] concrete reinforced bunkers,' recalled one SOG team leader. 'I personally found some abandoned base camps acres in size.' Bamboo and thatch storehouses brimmed with food, ammunition and other supplies. There were barracks, small hospitals and underground bunkers and tunnel networks to protect against air attacks. Larger camps even boasted theatrical groups who entertained the troops with patriotic plays and songs.

Similar camps existed across the border in South Vietnam itself. They dotted the regions under communist control, like the Central Highlands, War Zones C and D north and west of Saigon, and the Rung Sat Special Zone of the Mekong Delta. War Zone C, for example, was a 1000-square-mile area along the Cambodian border northwest of Saigon which the communists had controlled for 20 years. The French had never been able to subdue the area, and the South Vietnamese had never tried. Most of the population were communist sympathizers, who supplied the VC with food, shelter, recruits, porters and money. Even the powerful rubber-plantation owners in the area paid taxes to the Vietcong.

Top left: *A US Infantryman pinpoints a hidden bamboo breathing tube protruding from an underground Vietcong hideout north of Duc Pho.*
Top right: *This camouflaged tunnel was discovered and destroyed by men of the 196th Light Infantry Brigade during Operation Attleboro in 1966.*
Above: *ARVN soldiers bring in a Vietcong prisoner captured in a raid in the Camau Peninsula.*

Allied Operation Van Buren was undertaken to deny the January 1966 rice harvest to the Vietcong.

Throughout the dense forests and jungles of War Zone C, sophisticated base camps were scattered, complete with supply depots, barracks, training facilities and hospitals. An extensive system of tunnels and bunkers, some fortified with concrete, provided protection against air attack. Besides being home base for the 101st NVA regiment and the crack 9th VC Division, War Zone C was also believed to contain the Central Office for South Vietnam (COSVN) – headquarters for the entire Vietcong organization in the South.

Unlike the traditional military headquarters complex envisioned by the Americans, COSVN was actually a mobile command structure consisting of widely dispersed sections that frequently moved to avoid detection. It controlled all VC military forces, which were divided into the same three categories as the old Vietminh. At the hamlet and village level were the part-time guerrillas, who worked their fields by day and conducted sabotage raids at night. Regional force at the district and province level consisted of companies of 75-150 men who were better-trained and -armed than the local guerrillas.

Main-force battalions of 250-500 men were the Vietcong's elite fighting force. Highly trained and politically motivated, they acted as mobile light infantry units armed with heavy machine guns, mortars, RPGs and recoilless rifles. They were stiffened by the addition of NVA regulars, usually trained experts in explosives, communications, heavy weapons and other specialties.

Most NVA regulars, however, remained in their own units, which operated mainly in the Central Highlands under supervision of the B-3 Front military field headquarters. In 1965 these NVA regulars met American units head-on for the first time in the war when they moved into the Ia Drang Valley to develop secure lines of communication and supply from the highlands to the lowland areas. The

outcome of the bloody encounter at Ia Drang would cause the North Vietnamese to revise their tactics of 'big-unit warfare.' The major proponent of this offensive strategy was General Nguyen Chi Thanh, the commander of COSVN, who had initiated the 1965 spring offensive. Thanh soon learned that his light infantry units could not withstand direct assaults on US airborne units, backed by heavy artillery and air support.

General Giap, recalling a similar tactical error he had made when he committed his main-force units against the French in the Red River Delta in 1951, called for a renewed emphasis on guerrilla tactics. The Central Committee resolved the dispute by endorsing the continued deployment of large NVA regular units to the South to counter the US troop buildup. But these units were to adopt guerrilla tactics – attacking only when they held a clear advantage, springing on the enemy in surprise attacks, then withdrawing rapidly to avoid the full impact of US firepower. This technique was inspired by Mao's dictum that 'The strategy of guerrilla war is to pit one man against ten but the tactics are to pit ten men against one.' Communist main-force units would fight a war of maneuver against US heliborne assault forces along the border regions, striking at times of their own choosing, then retreating back to the safety of their mountain and jungle sanctuaries. Smaller units would tie down ARVN troops in the rear areas by means of sabotage, ambush and political terrorism. The key to success was their ability to avoid battle on the enemy's terms by methods of concealment and mobility.

Traveling in small units, and bivouacing deep in the jungles to avoid detection, the VC became experts at concealment, using twigs and branches as camouflage and leaving no traces behind to alert enemy patrols to their presence. In populated areas they employed extensive tunnel networks and underground bunkers, or blended in with the local population to elude allied patrols. One of the largest such underground systems was in the Chu Chi district, 60 kilometers northwest of Saigon along Route One. Created during the war with the French, the system had been enlarged into a network of underground rooms and passageways that stretched for some 200 kilometers underneath area villages and hamlets. The tunnels connected storage rooms for supplies and ammunition and living quarters which were ventilated by bamboo air shafts. Entrances were camouflaged trap doors hidden in village huts, or holes dug beneath the water line in nearby river banks.

Locating and uncovering these tunnel networks was a difficult and tedious task. The Americans used German Shepherds to sniff out tunnel entrances, but the Vietcong countered by sprinkling US-issue mosquito repellant around the entrances to hide their scent, or placing American soap and cigarettes just inside the trap doors to make the dogs think only Americans were present. Once a tunnel was uncovered, the Americans sent in 'tunnel rats' to flush out any Vietcong and wire the system with explosives.

The Americans frequently tried to separate the Vietcong from their local support by mounting armed sweeps through communist-held areas, flushing out the guerrillas and destroying caches of

A trained 'tunnel rat' of the 196th Light Infantry Brigade checks out Vietcong tunnels discovered south of Dao Tinh in 1966.

supplies found in local villages and hamlets. One of the first such sweeps occurred in July 1965, when the US 3rd Marine Division, based 60 miles south of Danang at Chu Lai, moved against the Vietcong stronghold in the nearby Batangan Peninsula. The area was honeycombed with tunnels, mine fields, booby traps, secret caches of food and ammunition. Three of the villages in the area had been identified as 'combat villages,' which acted as bases for local guerrilla units and some 2000 main-force Vietcong.

In what was known as Operation Starlite, a force of 5-6000 Marines backed by heavy artillery, air support and naval gunfire swept through the area in an awesome display of firepower and mobility. At the end of the battle, the Marines claimed victory, citing 559 enemy dead, 129 prisoners and 127 captured weapons. But the victory was short-lived, as the Batangan Peninsula quickly reverted to its former status once the Marines withdrew. The battle demonstrated that the only way conventional forces could neutralize communist combat villages was to obliterate them.

An example of this more drastic approach occurred in January 1967 against the 'Iron Triangle,' an area of dense forests and marshy rice paddies northwest of Saigon, which had been under undis-

puted VC control since 1964. The Iron Triangle provided the guerrillas with a secure base from which they could harass the key transportation routes leading to the North from the capital, as well as housing the headquarters for military, political and terrorist activities in the Saigon area.

The village of Ben Suc, which formed the northwest corner of the Iron Triangle, was considered the hub of guerrilla activity there. It housed the VC's Long Nguyen secret base, which was in essence a fortified supply and political center for the area. The 3500 or so villagers, and the 2500 others living in three smaller hamlets nearby, were organized into four rear service companies acting as laborers and transportation workers for the guerrillas. One moved supplies in sampans along the Saigon River, another unloaded them and the two remaining companies stored the matériel in and around Ben Suc and in the nearby jungle. The immediate area around the village itself was heavily mined and booby-trapped. Three VC units – the 7th Battalion, 165th Regiment and the 61st Local Force Company – were reportedly based nearby.

On 8 January, 60 UH-1 'Huey slick ships' landed in and around the village at dawn, disgorging an entire US infantry battalion of 420 men in less than

A staff sargeant of the 3rd Training Brigade explains Vietcong use of a 200-pound mace in jungle warfare. The device is hung from a tree with a trip wire attached to it and can knock out a squad of men when released.

Above: *A fully equipped ARVN soldier in Danang, 1968.*
Right: *In 1967 growing numbers of large-scale search-and-destroy missions* *uncovered many enemy base camps, and demonstrated that Americans could penetrate long-held guerrilla sanctuaries.*

two minutes. The soldiers quickly took up blocking positions around Ben Suc, while helicopters mounted with loudspeakers hovered overhead, broadcasting the warning: 'You are surrounded by Republic of South Vietnam and allied forces. Do not run away or you will be shot as VC.' A South Vietnamese battalion was helilifted in to interrogate the villagers and search the huts and nearby forests for hidden caches of supplies. They uncovered carefully concealed storage rooms within some of the huts containing large quantities of rice, and unearthed caches of medical supplies hidden in the surrounding jungle. The search also uncovered a number of tunnel and bunker complexes which were destroyed with demolition charges.

More than 6000 people were rounded up within the village and from surrounding hamlets for interrogation. One hundred and six of these were held for further questioning, a quarter of them considered hard-core guerrillas. The remaining 5987 villagers were evacuated by boat and helicopter to a government resettlement camp.

Once the inhabitants were gone, bulldozers and demolition teams of the 1st Engineer Battalion moved in and razed the village. They also cleared a twenty-acre patch of scrub jungle in the southwest corner of the village. 'The place was so infested with tunnels,' claimed the engineer battalion commander, 'that as my dozers would knock over the stumps of trees, the VC would pop out from behind.' Finally, a large hole was scooped out of the ground in the center of the village and filled with 10,000 pounds of explosives, which were detonated

to collapse any tunnels that had not been detected. The village of Ben Suc no longer existed. The now-depopulated Iron Triangle was turned into a 'free-fire zone' for American artillery and aircraft to discourage the Vietcong from returning.

It was futile to try making conventional tactics fit an unconventional war by creating clear-cut front lines where none existed. In the process, the Americans disrupted the local economy and deprived farmers of their traditional homelands. Thousands of peasants were forcibly relocated into squalid resettlement camps, which put a further burden on the Saigon Government and did little to help its image throughout the countryside. Against more remote communist strongholds, far removed from populated areas, the Americans were able to unleash the full weight of their superior firepower. Base camps and supply areas in inaccessible areas that were uncovered by aerial reconnaissance or other intelligence means became the target of US air strikes, including 'Arc Light' raids by giant USAF B-52s, each loaded with as many as 100 750-pound bombs. A single B-52 could blast a path of destruction through the jungle a mile long and a quarter-mile wide.

Vietcong and NVA soldiers were initially terrified of the bombers, which they could not see or hear until it was too late. Flying overhead at 33,000 feet, th B-52s dropped their bombs through the clouds, shattering the silence with earth-shaking explosions that uprooted trees and penetrated bunkers. Initially, the only defensive instructions VC officers could offer their men was: 'Run, run very fast.'

Above: *Two US Marines of the 1st Regiment check a hut in Quang Tri Province during Operation Badger Tooth.*

While Arc Light missions wreaked havoc among VC and NVA units when they were on target, faulty and outdated intelligence and the communists' practice of constantly moving from place to place, often saw the B-52s achieving little more than splintering trees in the jungle in what critics sarcastically labelled 'matchstick missions.' The communists also began obtaining advance warning of Arc Light missions. Soviet trawlers cruising off the coast of Guam monitored B-52 take-offs at Anderson Air Force Base and relayed the information to Hanoi, which in turn alerted its units in the South by radio. Since the 2650-mile flight from Guam to South Vietnam took about nine hours, the communists had ample time to disperse their forces and supplies.

On the ground, the Americans employed their heliborne and air-cavalry units to mount large 'search-and-destroy' operations to uncover enemy base camps and force a battle with main-force units. These offensives demonstrated that the Americans were capable of mounting large-scale sweeps into long-held guerrilla sanctuaries. Sudden helicopter assaults gave them the mobility to strike virtually anywhere they chose, regardless of the terrain. The lavish use of artillery and air strikes provided an enormous advantage in firepower which the Vietcong could not hope to match.

At first, US airmobile sweeps demoralized the Vietcong. But the VC and NVA discovered ways to counter US technological advantages. The American practice of 'prepping' a helicopter landing zone prior to an assault with artillery and air strikes often tipped off the enemy, who hid in the jungle during the barrage and then took up positions around the landing zone, ready to ambush the helicopter assault teams. In combat, the communists learned to attack quickly and engage the enemy at close quarters, so that fighter-bombers and artillery could not be used

against them. Once they had achieved their tactical objective, they withdrew quickly, leaving a series of small ambush parties and booby-traps in their wake. But if the odds against them were too great, the communists merely sidestepped the American juggernaut and melted into the jungle, often crossing the border into Cambodia and Laos where the Americans couldn't follow. Once the Americans withdrew, they simply recrossed the border and reoccupied the same piece of real estate. A captured communist political indoctrination document, dated March 1966, equated the Americans' mobile search-and-destroy tactics to 'stabbing the water' with a sword. 'When the sword is pulled out, the water remains unchanged.'

Below: Trained Revolutionary Development team members help Vietnamese refugees build temporary shacks until permanent quarters can be constructed across the canal in background (1966).
Bottom: Laborers clear brush for a helipad to be used by the 1st Air Cavalry Division in 1965.

America's War: 1965-75

Previous pages: *A Vietcong bugle captured in the Ia Drang Valley signals Company B of the 1st Platoon to move out toward their objective in a nearby valley: 2 March 1966.*

Above: *A lone soldier marks his location for supporting aircraft.*

their mission as quickly hunting down and destroying enemy main-force units were soon cursing those black-pajama guerrillas who had eluded both the French and, more recently, the ARVN. They learned that with a few exceptions – like the US Marines' Operation Starlite at Van Tuong and the 1st Cavalry's battle at Ia Drang – the enemy refused to fight according to conventional US military doctrine. Eventually, the brass turned to the irregulars – the 'Green Beanies' as they had been irreverently called – whose previous CIDG experience as jungle fighters proved valuable for long-range reconnaissance and patrol (LRRP, or 'Lurp') missions.

The Special Forces were ready. The 5th Special Forces Group, Airborne (5th SFG) activated its headquarters at Nha Trang in October 1964, replacing the temporary six-month Special Forces billets. The group consisted of five 20-man C Teams (Special Forces battalion-equivalent), each with three B Teams. In turn, each B Team (company-equivalent) controlled four 12-man A Teams. Although its authorized strength peaked in 1969 at 3740 Green Berets, 5th SFG actually controlled some 45,000 irregular troops during the war, and worked in tandem with US and ARVN regulars, as well as Regional and Popular Forces (RF/PFs), the South Vietnamese militia units known as 'Ruff-Puffs.'

Since Operation Switchback began in 1962, plans had called for a phased 'conventionalization' of the CIDG program under joint US Special Forces-LLDB command. CIDG irregulars were to be transformed into regular South Vietnamese units (either LLDB or Ranger units), or into the Regional Forces. Many *Montagnards* resisted this change, as old native-Vietnamese antipathy lurked beneath the surface and presented a constant problem to Special-Forces 'advisors,' who often were forced to fill a leadership vacuum from Vietnamese LLDB, due to the officers' lack of command initiative or rapport with irregular *Montagnard* troops. Beginning in 1964, the process moved slowly; the CIDG remained essentially an irregular force. But its mission did change: the old hamlet militias were dropped, and the smaller strike forces were expanded.

CIDG training and organization stressed border surveillance and more offensive operations – an exertion of Special Forces 'strike-force' philosophy over the CIA's emphasis on village defense and political action. As aggressive hunters of the Vietcong and the NVA, the CIDG became the core element of an evolving 5th Special Forces concept of mobile strike forces. Fortified CIDG/Special Forces camps, located astride known communist infiltration and supply routes on the border, became MACV's 'eyes and ears,' emphasizing long-range patrol techniques to compensate for large gaps between CIDG border camps (through which the communists quickly learned to infiltrate). Mobile strike forces became necessary to ensure the survival of relatively isolated camps from concentrated VC or NVA attacks and to perform varied missions: rapid exploitation of small-unit contacts, reconnaissance-in-force operations, extraction of compromised recon teams and others.

A forerunner of the mobile strike-force concept was 'Eagle Flight,' formed in October 1964. This small airmobile strike force served as a ready-

'Americanization' of the Vietnam War in 1965 overshadowed what had been largely an unknown, unconventional conflict. While US Special Forces technically remained 'advisors' to the South Vietnamese, some Green Berets feared their irregular capabilities might be misused, or worse, ignored altogether, by the conventional-minded MACV brass in Saigon.

US commanders schooled in 'big-unit' warfare on the plains of Europe generally pursued mobile warfare as taught at West Point, adapting their large-scale tactics to the smaller Indochina stage, seeking to destroy the Vietcong in epic, set-piece battles. Many conventional soldiers resented the Special Forces and all elites, seeing them as Hollywood glamor boys best suited for recruiting purposes. This attitude prevailed particularly after all the fuss made over the Green Berets during the Kennedy counterinsurgency fad. Many questioned their value in a regular army that traditionally smothered the opposition with mobility, heavy firepower and superior technology.

Unconventional Forces Remain in the Field

Despite regular-army biases, Vietnam, as the French had discovered to their cost, was essentially a small-unit war best suited to unconventional operations. American combat commanders who saw reaction, ambush and raiding element supporting both CIDG and regular operations under direct 5th SFG command. The original Eagle Flight was formed in II Corps Tactical Zone (II CTZ) force and consisted of 5 Green Berets and 36 highly trained *Montagnards*. With its own helicopter airlift and UH-1 'Huey' gunships, an Eagle Flight group was capable of independent combat operations and was often used as a reserve force. In one combat action in November 1965, an Eagle Flight and a small 1st Air Cavalry Division unit ambushed and wiped out an NVA weapons company deep in the enemy's backyard. When the rest of the NVA battalion attacked the patrol base in a desperate night action, the *Montagnards* and the air cavalrymen held until relieved by larger 1st Cavalry helicopters.

The strike-force concept evolved further during the 1965 US-troop buildup with the formation of 'Apache Force' and 'Eagle Scout' units, both composite units of Special Forces and CIDG strikers. Apache Force oriented newly arrived US combat battalions in VC/NVA small-unit tactics, accompanying green battalions into the field during their initial combat operations. Apache Forces also performed a secondary mission as a multi-purpose reserve/reaction force, often conducting joint offensive operations with special Nung CIDG companies. Eagle Scouts were a combat reconnaissance unit like the Apache Force, employed as an air-mobile strike force – a concept that came into its own in Vietnam.

The daddy of mobile strike forces was the specially trained Nung CIDG battalion formed in Danang in 1965 as a mobile reserve for remote Special Forces/CIDG camps. To a Special-Forces soldier compromised behind the lines, a Nung striker was worth his weight in gold. The Nungs – brawny ethnic Chinese – were a tribe from northern Vietnam that had fought hard for the French and received high marks as professional soldiers. In fact, the French organized a full Nung division (later disbanded by the South Vietnamese for security reasons). Nungs had immigrated south by the thousands after the communist takeover, settling in the Central Highlands.

Nungs were renowned jungle fighters, highly valued by the CIA and Special Forces for their combat prowess in the CIDG program and hired at top pay to serve as bodyguards for Special Forces. The Nungs often held many CIDG units together in the heat of combat, as at Nam Dong in July 1964. Although the CIDG as a whole were often referred to as mercenaries (for military service, they were paid like any other soldiers), only the Nungs could be truly called mercenaries, as they were trained, fed, paid and led by the Americans; in return, the Nungs devoted themselves loyally to the Americans, as they had to the French.

In June 1965, MACV authorized the formation of Mobile Strike Force Commands (MSFCs) in each of the four Corps Tactical Zones (CTZ) and at the 5th SFG Nha Trang HQ. These five 'MIKE' forces combined the various strike-force missions under 5th SFG command. The brigade-sized MIKE force consisted of a permanent A detachment, several 552-man CIDG striker battalions, a 135-man reconnaissance company and an elite 227-man headquarters/service company staffed by either airborne-

qualified Nungs (in the Central Highlands) or ethnic Khmers (Cambodians, called 'Bodes by Special Forces, located farther south). All MIKE force companies contained a 34-man combat recon platoon and were rapidly airmobile for any contingency.

The 5th MSFC (Detachment B-55) was the largest MIKE force (2570 men by 1968), with nearly 60 percent airborne-qualified. Although primarily intended for ready reaction missions, the 5th MSFC saw action in all four CTZs under the group commander's operational control. All MSFCs were under 5th SFG control until December 1966, when they were brought under joint US-Vietnamese control. Reinforcing missions were extended to non-Special-Force units as required, and the 5th MSFC was capable of extended combat in brigade-sized operations. The 4th MSFC (B-40), located at Don Phuc in the Mekong Delta, operated from floating

Top: *ARVN soldiers aboard a CH-21 helicopter await the signal that they have arrived over the drop area.*
Above: *Phnom Penh, Cambodia, as seen from a 1st Marine Brigade helicopter flying in to evacuate refugees from the Khmer Rouge takeover in 1975.*

Top left: *Popular Forces troops join the 25th Infantry Division for a search-and-destroy sweep in the Pleiku area in February 1967.*
Bottom left: *Two Kit Carson Scouts indicate the location of suspected enemy installations near Danang to US Marines.*
Opposite top: *A well-camouflaged member of a US Navy SEAL team watches intently for any movement along a thickly wooded stream bank.*
Opposite bottom: *The* Montagnards, *shunned by lowland Vietnamese, proved themselves valuable allies to both French and American troops.*

helicopter and patrol bases in the rivers and maintained a company of swift airboats armed with 30-caliber machine guns for rapid mobility in swampy delta terrain.

By 1966 MIKE forces represented a quantum leap in military capability from the black-pajama irregulars of the early CIDG program, armed with old Springfield rifles and Swedish 'K' submachine guns. The new MIKE forces were jump-qualified, wore steel helmets and camouflage jungle fatigues and carried M-16 automatic rifles. MIKE forces could travel through the jungle as swiftly as any Vietcong or NVA Main-Force unit (often faster). While Main-Force NVA and Vietcong found the lightly armed MIKE forces more of an equal match than conventional US units, MIKE-force mobility meant quick reaction to any communist attempt to overrun one of 80 far-flung Special Forces border camps all over South Vietnam.

Long-Range Reconnaissance Patrols

Another priority of 5th SFG was the development of long-range reconnaissance patrol (Lurp) capabilities for 'strategic recon' – special intelligence on enemy troop movements in communist-controlled territory. Project Delta (Detachment B-52) originated in May 1964 as SOG's covert Project Leaping Lena in order to train CIDG and Vietnamese LLDB in long-range reconnaissance tactics. When the 5th Special Forces Group inherited the LRRP mission in May 1965 (at the same time Blackburn claimed all covert cross-border operations as SOG's domain alone), Leaping Lena became Project Delta. It specialized in LRRP intelligence collection, placement of air-strikes or artillery on North Vietnamese and Viet-cong bases, and conduct of various 'special ops.' Delta's intelligence function differed from the traditional LRRP mission, which was restricted to the FEBA (Forward Edge of Battle Area), a distance usually within reach of the parent division's artillery range. Delta, on the other hand, pioneered strategic reconnaissance, which required infiltration of enemy territory, far outside the artillery umbrella, to collect information on the enemy's intentions and capabilities. (Communist units rarely strayed into the artillery umbrella of a regular US combat battalion.) Delta teams could roam the countryside collecting intelligence for the highest command

levels. If it engaged in a firefight with superior communist forces, or located a major communist target, Delta called for airstrikes from available carrier-borne Navy jets, Army helicopter gunships, or Air Force tactical-support aircraft.

Special Forces troops assigned to Delta were considered the elite of elites. Delta consisted of 450 men organized into 12 recon teams, 6 (later 12) 'Roadrunner' teams, a camp Nung security company and a full-time reaction force, the 91st ARVN Ranger Battalion, which included several companies of highly trained and dependable Nungs. For the tricky heliborne infiltration of its recon teams, Delta (and other strategic recon projects) relied on the 281st Helicopter Assault Company, which usually supported Delta operations. Crews of the 281st often slept on their choppers, prepared to lift off at a moment's notice, their gunships often so loaded down with rockets and ammo that the pilots skipped or bounced several times to get aloft. The chopper pilots were completely integrated into Delta operations, even wearing tiger suits, Delta triangle patches and .38 revolvers on their hips. Special Air Force FAC (Forward Air Controller) units and even US Marine Corps airmen were also assigned to Delta on a full-time basis. So valuable did conventional military commanders find Delta's strategic intelligence that at one point USMC Lt General Robert Cushman assigned the 1st Marine Air Wing – commanded by a major general – to opcon (operational control) of Delta's commander, a mere army major.

'Roadrunners' were all-Vietnamese and indigenous-force units dressed in NVA uniforms or

Vietcong black pajamas. Their mission was to mingle with the NVA/VC (sometimes carrying a Swedish 'K' under their shirts and a concealed grenade), report their positions, or lead them into Delta ambushes. Roadrunners would report to an enemy unit, infiltrate a meeting of the command unit, blast away with a submachine gun and dive back into the bush. Such dangerous missions resulted in an understandable shortage of Roadrunner volunteers.

Extraction of Delta's compromised teams was also a hazardous undertaking, requiring brave and

Above: *An F-4J Phantom II fighter comes in for a landing on the aircraft carrier USS* Constellation *in the South China Sea.*

skilled chopper pilots to pluck teams from triple-canopy jungle by STABO and McGuire rigs – specially designed harnesses that enabled extraction of several men, even wounded, simultaneously and under fire. Many times, recon teams would 'exfil' dangling from choppers until pilots could touch down in safe territory. Many a firebase commander was totally confused at the sight of unmarked Delta 'blackbirds' landing in their perimeters to load up Vietnamese in NVA uniforms, departing without so much as a word.

Delta personnel infiltrated enemy areas so completely that they often could hear NVA troops conversing on trails. Roadrunners and other Delta members also confused the enemy in his own backyard, which was their purpose. NVA troopers were known to have approached Delta's indigenous personnel to ask directions or make conversation without realizing their error – until too late. After Delta located and called in airstrikes on NVA positions, special Nung bomb-damage assessment platoons returned to count bodies and equipment.

Delta also co-ordinated operations with regular combat units, as in the relief of Plei Me CIDG camp in October 1965. At the time, Delta's commander was Major Charles 'Chargin' Charlie' Beckwith, another legendary Special-Forces trooper. Beckwith was a Southern 'good ol' boy' with an ample supply of guts and resources (legend has a young Beckwith running an occasional load of home-brewed 'white lightning' liquor in the back hills of Georgia). A University of Georgia football hero and ROTC officer who had been drafted by the Green Bay Packers, Beckwith chose the US Army instead. A friend commented years later that Beckwith 'was playing on a bigger team as far as he was concerned.'

Beckwith served in the 82nd Airborne Division, 77th Special Forces Group, and in Bull Simons' White Star teams in Laos. In 1962 Beckwith was one of two US Special-Forces members selected to go on a year-long exchange program with the 22nd Special Air Service (SAS), part of Britain's renowned commando units. Beckwith's year included an unofficial tour with the SAS hunting communist guerrilla remnants in Malaya. Beckwith returned convinced that the US Army needed an elite SAS type of unit. His detailed proposal was pigeonholed by the army bureaucracy. Still he persisted. 'We're going to have a unit like that in this army,' he told comrades. 'I'm going to be the guy to organize it and I'm going to command it.' Delta was a good place to start. He began attracting the best men to Delta by sending out flyers to all Special-Forces camps: 'Wanted – Volunteers for Project DELTA. Will Guarantee You Two Things: a Medal, A Body Bag, or Both.'

Beckwith took over Delta as NVA regulars began pouring into South Vietnam; at the same time, MACV began building up American regulars, and demanded Delta's strategic recon. Beckwith's recon teams turning up unmistakable evidence of increased communist military capabilities. At Plei Me, however, Delta uncovered the biggest find of the war to that time: offensive operations by hard-core NVA regulars in regimental strength. One American officer remembered that 'These weren't the black-pajama boys who run when they see you coming.' NVA regulars wore helmets, uniforms, webbed gear and certainly were not running from any fight.

In October 1965 the 33rd NVA Regiment besieged Plei Me CIDG camp, a triangular border outpost 25 miles west of Pleiku, while the 32nd NVA Regiment waited to ambush the expected ARVN relief column. Communist mortars closed the camp from helicopter resupply and evacuation, isolating its 12 Americans and 300 *Montagnard* defenders. Dropped outside Plei Me, Beckwith personally led two companies of Delta Rangers to Plei Me, infiltrating the tight NVA ring around the camp. At daylight Beckwith charged his men into the camp through a hail of machine-gun fire and, taking command, strengthened Plei Me's defenses. Beckwith's men confirmed the existence of NVA regulars and held the camp until relief by 1st Air Cavalry troops, which chased the NVA into the Ia

Main picture: *A heavily armed A-7 Corsair II is launched from the USS* Ranger *for an air strike over North Vietnam.*

Below: *An aerial view of the thermal power plant at Hanoi, target of a 1973 Linebacker mission.*

Above: *Lieutenant General William C Westmoreland*.

rank, with a previous Vietnam tour and experience in a special project dealing with long-range reconnaissance.

The school's three-week training course was grueling, with elimination rate among the two cycles of 60 men each exceeding 30 percent. Curriculum consisted of map reading, aerial photo analysis, emergency medical aid, proficiency in PRC-25 field radio, nomenclature and specs of enemy weapons, immediate action drills and sabotage. Students learned important jungle fighting techniques, rapelling, concealment and security, sound and smell recognition. Recondo School's 'final exam' was a five-day recon patrol in VC territory. Apparently, the course was successful: between November 1966 and April 1968, only two combat deaths occurred during these 'graduation' missions, although enemy contacts were common, especially during the 1968 Tet Offensive. By mid-1967 the Recondo School had trained 73 Special-Forces combat platoons and numerous other regular-force LRRP specialists.

Regular Force Elites

Despite the success of the special recon projects, SOG unconventional operations, and the Recondo School, the irregular warfare concept was not applied to conventional units on a large scale. Even ARVN, composed of Vietnamese who should have been more comfortable in the field than American irregulars, remained very much a reflection of its conventional US training and equipment. ARVN was losing the war when American combat forces began to arrive in June 1965, despite the fact that ARVN regulars totaled 227,000, with over 325,000 men in paramilitary units. American combat forces, eventually totaling over 500,000 troops, came in ostensibly to relieve ARVN of heavy combat duties and allow them to focus on pacification duties at the village level, but American regulars fared little better, merely performing search-and-destroy missions more aggressively than ARVN.

Americans tended to rate ARVN combat capabilities poorly. Even among elite ARVN units, combat performance varied. Many US Special Forces held the Vietnamese LLDB in low regard (although many individual soldiers performed well), and some units were considered no good at all. There were exceptions, however. Although elite units did not possess the same *élan* as, say, the British-trained Gurkhas (although the Nung mercenaries came very close to them), some units, when offered superb leadership and professional motivation, were as tough as any troops in the world. Such units as the 8th Airborne Battalion at Tan Son Nhut had a macho mentality that buoyed morale and led troops to feel they would win in battle. Recruitment for such units was no problem, despite the higher casualty rates among them. Many volunteers were either ex-North Vietnamese or sons of 1954 refugees – men with strong motivation to resist communism.

ARVN Airborne Rangers, armored units and Vietnamese Marines usually could be counted on for a good fight. One of the toughest under fire was the ARVN 52nd Ranger Battalion, which recruited men who chose military service over prison from Saigon jails. 'These guys were killers,' recalled an American advisor; 'I never saw any of them run.' The elites

Drang Valley for the first major battle between American and North Vietnamese regulars – a stunning American victory. Beckwith's unit later conducted strategic recon in the A Shau Valley – a traditional NVA hornet's nest – for the 1st Cav. Beckwith lost several recon teams (he himself was badly wounded charging in to rescue a compromised team), but Delta indicated the presence of large NVA forces.

Impressed by Delta's performance, General Westmoreland authorized two more unconventional-warfare special recon projects, Sigma (Detachment B-56) and Omega (Detachment B-50), in 1966. Omega and Sigma – nicknamed 'the Greeks' – were smaller than Delta (about 900 CIDG/ARVN and 125 US Special Forces) and operated under exclusive US command. The larger Delta organization had capability to deploy in any CTZ, as directed by the ARVN and MACV. Sigma was located at Ho Ngoc Tau in III CTZ and used ethnic Cambodians and Chinese troops. Omega was located at Ban Me Thuot in II CTZ and employed *Montagnard* tribesmen, Cham and ethnic Chinese minorities.

In September 1966, Westmoreland gave Delta the additional mission of training regular US infantry, ARVN Rangers, CIDG and Vietnamese LLDB units in LRRP tactics at the MACV Reconnaissance and Commando (Recondo) School at Nha Trang. Westmoreland, a strong backer of unconventional LRRP tactics in support of regular units, had initiated the Recondo concept in the 101st Airborne Division in 1958, and revived LRRP training based on Project Delta's field performance. The school was located at Nha Trang, adjacent to Delta's compound, and served all MACV commands. Colonel Francis J Kelly, 5th SFG commander, held operational control and provided many of the carefully chosen instructors – at least E-7 (Master Sergeant) in

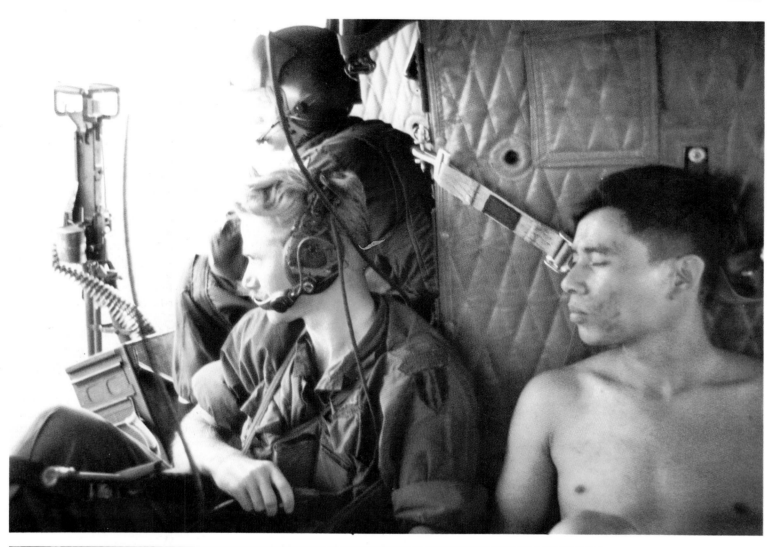

Above: *A captured Vietcong is brought in by members of the 21st Signal Company in 1970.*
Left: *A Vietnamese interpreter shows a crippling Vietcong foot trap to members of the 173rd Airborne Brigade at Vong Cam Dia.*

Above: *A US Navy
monitor boat in the Mekong
Delta uses flamethrowers to
destroy possible enemy
ambush sites along a
stream.*

*A river patrol boat (PBR)
makes its rounds along the
heavily traveled Mekong
River.*

tended to be well led and equipped. Unfortunately,
elite forces represented only about 5 percent of total
South Vietnamese forces, with much of the balance
conscripts.

American elites also constituted a small part of
total US troop strengths (a commitment of over
500,000 at 1968 peak), but adapted well to the
demands in the field for special capabilities. An
excellent example of a military unit adapting to local
conditions was that of the US Marine Corps special-
recon units that spearheaded the Marines' deep
reconnaissance efforts in Vietnam. Recon Marines
served as raiders, conducted clandestine helicopter
insertions and saw combat near the Lao border in I
CTZ with Vietnamese LLDB and Special Forces/
CIDG units.

At the Nha Trang Recondo School, selected
American and ARVN Rangers, CIDG and LLDB
troops were trained in LRRP tactics to give both
regular and irregular units a built-in long-range
recon capability. Special LRRP Ranger units became integral to US regular combat battalions (although engaged in long-range recon at the FEBA,
rather than the strategic recon of the special projects). Besides the Ranger 'Lurp' platoons, 'Kit
Carson Scouts' worked closely with US combat
forces; these were ex-communists who had defected
through the *Chieu Hoi* (Open Arms) program and
were expert at directing Americans past communist
ambushes and booby traps, and uncovering arms
and rice caches.

US Navy SEALs, the Navy's elite special warfare
troops, operated in a variety of unconventional
roles. The first SEAL platoons to arrive in the
country in 1966 staked out the marshy Mekong
Delta as their natural habitat, turning the old Run
Sat swamps (the former Binh Xuyen stronghold)
into a special operating zone. SEAL Teams One and
Two set up surveillance posts and mounted three-
man hunter-killer raids into Vietcong safe areas.
SEALs operated with US Navy Task Force 116 –
the American successor to the old French *dinassauts*
– and proved instrumental in wresting control over
much of the Mekong Delta from the Vietcong. Like
the VC, SEAL 'green-faced frogmen' were noctur-
nal creatures who infiltrated and raided VC areas by
various means, including Swift airboats and Seawolf
helicopters.

SEAL teams performed aquatic missions for a
variety of sponsors: Task Force 116, SOG, CIA's
Phoenix Program. In combined operations with
Special Forces/CIDG units, SEALs operated from
'floating camps' in the Mekong Delta, complete
with bunkers and helipads built on floating floors
for year-round operation. SEAL/CIDG airboats,

motorized sampans and choppers could attack Vietcong sanctuaries even during the monsoon season, which restricted most offensive operations.

Task Force 116's riverine operations – one area in which the Americans learned valuable lessons from the French experience – gained non-communist forces access to the very heart of South Vietnam's populated rice bowl. TF 116's operations, code-named Game Warden, began in 1965 with a motley collection of 24 old French-converted LCM monitors (which had begun their military career as World War II US Surplus landing craft). In time, Game Warden's 'brown-water navy' had over 750 vessels, including 450 8-ton fiberglass river patrol boats (PBRs) – driven by water-jets and armed with twin .50-caliber machine guns forward and a .30-caliber mounted aft. Other components were armored troop carriers (ATCs) to ferry assault troops up inland waterways and fast-patrol air-cushioned vehicles (PACVs). US Navy riverine troops wore distinctive black berets. By 1968 Game Warden's Mobile Riverine Force ran four heavily armed river assault squadrons. Game Warden squadrons and SEAL flotillas patrolled the Mekong with a brigade of the 9th Infantry Division, a composite amphibious force of tremendous firepower and mobility when projected deep into the Vietcong's Mekong sanctuaries.

Market Time Operations along coastal water-ways, beginning in 1965, denied to the communists seaborne infiltration and logistical supply along some 1000 miles of South Vietnamese coastline. Market Time used US Navy and Coast Guard pickets to spot potential infiltrators among 50,000 junks and sampans engaged in daily fishing and trade. Communist infiltration by sea accounted for 70 percent of VC supplies before 1965, but no more than 10 percent as a result of Market Time. The successor operations, Coronado (1967-8) and SEA LORDS (for South East Asia Lake/Ocean/River Delta Strategy, 1968-9), denied the Vietcong exclusive use of inland and coastal waterways, accounting for the combat deaths of over 2500 Vietcong and the capture of hundreds of tons of war matériel.

One of the least-known special units was the Air Force Aerospace Rescue and Recovery Service (ARRS). The outfit's pararescue specialists, trained as medics, paratroopers, frogmen and Rangers, were constantly prepared for any contingency involving downed US flyers whether in North or South Vietnam, Cambodia, or Laos. The first ARRS team arrived in 1962 and used borrowed Army or Marine Corps choppers. As the air war against the North accelerated in 1965, ARRS flew in specially equipped HH-3E 'Jolly Green Giant' helicopters and HU-16 amphibious aircraft, operating out of Danang for rescue of downed pilots in the Gulf of Tonkin. In June 1966, the 3rd ARRS Group

A US Navy Neptune surveillance plane overflies a Vietnamese junk during Market Time operations south of Vung Tau (1966).

was activated at Tan Son Nhut for rescue operations all over Southeast Asia (although the services continued to mount their own local rescue operations). ARRS choppers often penetrated North Vietnamese airspace as necessary to pick up downed aircrew. Although no more than 125 ARRS pararescuemen (nicknamed PJs) were ever in Indochina at one time, between 1962 and 1975 ARRS saved 3883 men while losing 71 PJs and 45 aircraft to enemy fire.

Unconventional & Guerrilla Operations

Special recon projects advanced the strike-force concept toward independent long-range irregular task forces called Mobile Guerrilla Forces (MGFs). The MGFs consisted of a 12-man Special Forces A team cadre, a 150-man mobile guerrilla company (usually indigenous MIKE forces trained in guerrilla warfare) and a 34-man combat recon platoon. Like the old French GCMAs, mobile guerrillas operated in remote areas deep behind communist lines for extended periods, conducting enemy surveillance, reconnaissance, sabotage and interdiction.

Mobile Guerrilla Force operations, begun at the instigation of 5th SFG commander Colonel Francis 'Blackjack' Kelly, for whom they were code-named, commenced in October 1966 with Blackjack 21 (for II CTZ, 1st operation). Led by SF Captain J A Fenlon, the operation took 250 *Montagnards* deep into Kontum Province on a 30-day patrol. A month later the mobile guerrillas emerged from the jungle hotly pursued by two Vietcong Main-Force battalions. Another MGF operation, Blackjack 33 (April-May 1967), commanded by Captain James 'Bo' Gritz, employed Project Sigma's recon elements and resulted in 320 confirmed enemy KIA (killed in action).

MGF/Blackjack personnel, like the special recon projects, were airborne-qualified, trained in special weapons, silent movement and tracking, and wound treatment. Each operation was carefully planned and detailed before launch, so that each guerrilla felt secure in the mission and contingency plans. Guerrilla teams never took large casualties behind enemy lines, a credit to team planning and execution, and usually succeeded in accomplishing their assigned missions.

These irregulars possessed the same tenacity, mobility and deceptive tactics that made the VC so effective against conventional US forces. They always strove to hit first, hit hard and melt back into the jungle. With normal resupply impossible deep in the enemy-controlled jungle, MGF were supplied by USAF Air Commandos, who dropped dummy 500-lb napalm canisters during actual airstrikes, so as not to reveal guerrilla positions. In mid-1967 Mobile Guerrilla Forces and MIKE Forces, with their respective missions, were integrated into Mobile Strike Force Commands (MSFCs).

Opposite top: A US Navy inshore patrol craft (PCE) makes a high-speed run near the Vietnamese coastline.
Below: Members of the 'brown water navy' disembark from their patrol craft to invade a Vietcong stronghold on Tan Dinh Island during Operation Bold Dragon III.
Below right: A Chinese operator and a CIDG soldier learn the use of an air boat from Special Forces personnel at Can Tho.

The Green Beret Murder Case

A particular problem among the 80-odd camps under 5th SFG command was the need for critical intelligence and counterintelligence on a full-time basis. MACV J-2 (Intelligence) received information from 5th SFG camps, especially on enemy buildups, but 5th SFG camps themselves suffered from lack of information about the 'big picture' (what to look for on patrols and local threats to the camps). Many camps developed their own intelligence agents among local peasants, mostly to warn of impending VC attack. Meanwhile, communist agents also infiltrated Special Forces camps, and a good SF commander assumed that his local strikers had been penetrated by VC agents who provided enemy troops with a camp's layout, strongpoints and weaknesses. Green Berets and Vietnamese LLDB insulated themselves somewhat by living in separate inner compounds surrounded by wire and guarded by loyal Nungs. Camp fortifications were also wired for demolition in case disloyal CIDG troops turned against the Americans or LLDB.

As a precaution, 5th SFG encouraged development of counterintelligence networks. In 1967 5th SFG designated Project Gamma (Detachment B-57) to organize cross-border counterintelligence nets on

the buildup of NVA bases and infiltration trails (the Ho Chi Minh Trail in Laos and its Cambodian version, the 'Sihanouk Trail') that supported NVA/VC attacks on CIDG camps. Gamma's 52-man detachment hired South Vietnamese agents to actually collect information. These agents were strictly Gamma employees; the South Vietnamese Government knew nothing of B-57's secret intelligence nets.

By 1969 Gamma intelligence networks were credited with providing timely information that saved many American and ARVN lives. But in May 1969, the communists began rolling up B-57's agent networks along the Cambodian border at an alarming rate. An intensive investigation by Gamma's veteran intelligence officers narrowed the field to a single sector managed by a South Vietnamese agent. His interrogation (which Special Forces histories insist employed legal methodologies, such as lie detectors and truth serum) revealed the man to be a North Vietnamese double agent. When the subject disappeared suddenly in June 1969, US Army investigators charged seven 5th SFG intelligence officers with his murder.

The highly publicized 'Green Beret murder case' never went to trial because the CIA, which worked with 5th SFG counterintelligence officers, refused to testify on its sources and methods. But this incident, plus other controversy surrounding subsequent counterintelligence operations like Phoenix, was a black eye for the Special Forces, tarnishing the Green Berets' once spotless reputation with the general public.

Concurrent with the development of Mobile Guerrilla Forces, SOG expanded OPLAN 35, its covert cross-border operations. In late 1965, Prairie

Fire operations succeeded Shining Brass in Laos; in 1966, SOG added cross-border missions into Cambodia, code-named Daniel Boone. Expanded SOG operations were promoted by Colonel Blackburn's successor, Colonel John K Singlaub (SOG commander April 1966-7). Singlaub also had previous experience of unconventional combat; during World War II he had organized Chinese guerrillas along the Sino-Vietnamese border. Singlaub raised SOG personnel levels to 2500 Americans and over 7000 Vietnamese and indigenous soldiers, and reorganized their operations. Until 1966 these had been launched from four operating bases (FOBs): at Phu Bai, Kontum, Khe Sanh and Danang. Singlaub consolidated SOG into three outfits, each responsible for a specific area of operations: Command & Control North (CCN) covered North Vietnam and Laos from Danang; Command & Control Central (CCC) the tri-border region of Vietnam/Laos/Cambodia from Kontum in II CTZ; and Command & Control South (CCS) for Cambodia operations from Ban Me Thuot in III CTZ. Recon Teams became 'Spike' teams composed of three Special-Forces and nine indigenous troops. Exploitation forces were given the name 'Hatchet Forces,' made up of four Green Berets and 30 indigenous troops, and used for larger-scale over-the-fence missions. Finally, Singlaub created several larger company-sized reserve-reaction forces called SLAM (Search-Locate-Annihilate-Monitor) companies, which Spike and Hatchet teams could call on when in trouble.

Calls from compromised SOG teams could be relayed from a secret SOG radio outpost in Laos known as Eagle's Nest. Personally reconnoitered by Singlaub, Eagle's Nest rested atop one of the area's highest peaks, chosen for its defensibility. SOG personnel successfully defended the outpost against repeated NVA attacks during the war. After 1967 all Special-Forces soldiers posted to SOG for clandestine missions were given a 5th-SFG cover designation: 'Special Operations Augmentation (SOA), 5th Special Forces Group.'

After Singlaub pushed and pulled for expanded missions, SOG teams ranged all over Indochina, including operations code-named Kit Cat, which entered North Vietnam in 1968. These extra-sensitive missions were sharply limited to intelligence-gathering (no military operations – ambush, sabotage, etc, allowed), with team information relayed via special communications centers like Eagle's Nest, or by stations at Tri Bach, near Hué. These beamed the coded message directly to Saigon or to the supersecret National Security Agency (NSA) headquarters in Fort Belvoir, Maryland.

The North Vietnamese greatly improved their ability to locate and track SOG teams, whose dangerous missions became even tougher as the war reached full pitch in 1968. Infiltrated by blackbird choppers into Laos or Cambodia, SOG's Spike teams often uncovered surprises. On one mission, in February 1968, nine-man Spike Team Maine, led by Staff Sergeant Fred Zabitosky, dropped into triple-jungle canopy and ten-foot elephant grass near Attopeu, Laos, accidentally landing on top of a 2000-man NVA division headquarters. Spike Team Maine included six Nungs (two veterans, aged 47 and 54, had fought under the French) and two first-

time Americans. Zabitosky himself was a veteran of two previous Vietnam tours, the first with an A-Team in a CIDG camp, and later on SOG's OPLAN 34A 'marops' (martime operations). He had also completed 13 cross-border operations into Laos and Cambodia.

Zabitosky's team was under heavy fire from the moment the choppers pulled pitch and lifted out. The American sergeant radioed for help as he directed a fierce firefight from all sides. The first chopper took out several Nungs, while Zabitosky, the remaining Nungs and the Americans jumped onto the second. Almost a hundred feet in the air, the chopper was blown from the sky by a rocket-propelled grenade, hurling Zabitosky to the ground, crushing his ribs. As A1-E Skyraiders strafed the LZ (Landing Zone), the dazed American staggered to the burning chopper and pulled out the pilot and co-pilot before the ship's fuel cells exploded. A rescue chopper finally picked up the three men at a second LZ. Spike Team Maine's nine men reportedly killed 165 NVA regulars in two LZs. Zabitosky received the Congressional Medal of Honor a year later, but owing to the clandestine nature of this mission, his citation recorded his bravery in Vietnam. Over 15 years later, the Army does not acknowledge that Zabitosky's heroic incident took place in Laos.

Above: *Two CIDG advisors accompany their men on an operation from Camp Thuong Duc in 1967.*
Opposite top: *A US Navy crew chief with an M-60 machine gun surveys a Delta village from his UH-1B Iroquois helicopter.*
Right: *South Vietnamese soldiers on a covert mission in Laos seek out enemy supply depots and bunkers for destruction.*

One of SOG's missions under Singlaub became known as 'prisoner snatch,' the capture of NVA prisoners to interrogate for intelligence purposes. Spike teams used smaller-caliber pistols to incapacitate, rather than kill. For the capture of a live NVA soldier, SOG offered lucrative bonuses, such as R&R for the Americans and cash bounties for native troops. It was a challenge, but a difficult one, as a 'snatch' risked compromising a team's location. Only 50 NVA prisoners were successfully snatched in Laos and Cambodia during the war.

SOG missions, while extremely dangerous, never lacked volunteers; their American leaders, expert in unconventional operations, usually fared well. Only 103 American Special Forces were killed in 2675 SOG cross-border activities between 1965 and 1972. Like the old GCMAs, SOG, mobile guerrillas and the special projects brought the war directly to the communists. Although their main task was to collect strategic intelligence for MACV and regular combat units, just as important was their psychological impact on the enemy. These irregulars kept the communist soldier off-balance: doubtful of the 'safe' trail just ahead; wary that the next mortar round might be rigged (by SOG's Project Eldest Son) to explode in his face; or that the 'comrade' sharing his rice at a rest station could be a CIDG roadrunner. The objective was to deny the enemy his previous sense of security in the bush.

Rescue and Recovery Operations

Besides highly classified special projects, the most difficult and dangerous unconventional missions were rescue and recovery operations. One of the most secret and daring recovery missions of the war occurred in December 1966, when 5th SFG Captain 'Bo' Gritz took his 1st Mobile Guerrilla Force – 12 Americans and 250 Cambodian mercenaries – across the Cambodian border to recover the 'black box' from a downed U-2 spyplane. The U-2 strategic reconnaissance plane was the same high-flying type that the Soviet Union had shot down in 1960, capturing CIA pilot Colonel Gary Powers. U-2 aircraft routinely operated over Southeast Asia – some out of CIA's secret base-within-a-base in Udorn, Thailand – but none had ever crashed in enemy territory. President Johnson had personally ordered the recovery of the black box to prevent its secret codes from falling into Soviet hands (the device had failed to self-destruct on impact). The Air Force could offer only a remote clue as to where the plane had crashed – a conical area encompassing some 440 square miles of VC-infested territory. Westmoreland gave the job of recovery to 5th SFG's Colonel 'Blackjack' Kelly, who turned to Gritz. 'It's suicide,' he told Kelly, 'but if you want to try it, I should be the one.'

Bo Gritz was a tough Special-Forces man, who, like Charlie Beckwith (under whom Gritz had served with Delta at Plei Me), was considered a 'do-anything' type of soldier. He had a reputation as a 'howl-at-the-moon wildman,' held a black belt in karate, could jump out of a plane at 20,000 feet, freefall almost four miles, pop his chute at 700 feet and land on a dime. He had joined Special Forces in 1957, after turning down a West Point appointment, and served three Vietnam tours.

Gritz and his 'Bodes pulled out all the stops to recover the black box. Choppers dropped the guerrilla strike force at the border, where Gritz fanned out his teams to search for a needle in a haystack. His guerrillas made painfully slow progress in the tall elephant grass and tangled vines, leaving booby traps behind to cover their rear. The border region was also crawling with VC. 'It was a running gun battle from the word Go,' Gritz recalled.

After three days of playing hide-and-seek in the jungle, one of Gritz's 'Bodes found the wrecked aircraft, only to discover the black box missing. Gritz figured the VC had carted it off, recognizing its value. His troops set an ambush along a well-worn trail to catch a prisoner. As his men blasted the next VC patrol, Gritz and a Green Beret sergeant collared

Main picture: *CH-53 Sea Stallion Marine helicopters carry out evacuation exercises in Phnom Penh, Cambodia, only days before the country fell to the communists.*

Inset: *A North Vietnamese Army training center uncovered in Cambodia in 1970 yielded these models of US aircraft used as training aids.*

A firefight at Long Dinh pins down three troopers of the 11th Armored Cavalry.

the two point men, but Gritz accidentally killed his prisoner with a CIA-supplied 'zapper' – a lethal spring-steel billyclub. The NCO only wounded his man, who confirmed Gritz's hunch and led his troops to the VC encampment. The American-led guerrillas crashed through the perimeter with total surprise, shot their way in, located the precious black box and shot their way out, retreating into the dark jungle. Gritz didn't lose a man.

The Cambodian operation went so well that Gritz took his 'Bodes into Cambodia again on a Blackjack mission, raided 53 VC bases in 60 days and lost only one man. His successes led SOG to initiate the Daniel Boone cross-border operations into Cambodia. Recalling his secret black-box mission years later, Gritz remarked that 'We came out of the jungle feeling like Daniel Boone.'

Another famous operation, the November 1970 raid into North Vietnam to rescue American POWs, was not so successful. As America's role in the Vietnam War wound down, the Pentagon's concern over the POWs increased, as Hanoi made very clear its intention to use the POWs as hostages, 'bargaining chips' for continued US troop withdrawals from Vietnam. In addition, public awareness of the plight of US POWs was at an all-time high. The JCS had long considered a POW rescue operation, and in early 1970 ordered former SOG commander, now Brigadier General, Blackburn, to study the possibility of a dramatic POW rescue. Blackburn realized the difficulty of such missions. US troops had secretly conducted numerous but largely unsuccessful POW rescue operations in South Vietnam. The only American POW successfully freed from a VC prison

camp later died of wounds inflicted by his captors during the rescue. Air Force ARRS teams and SOG operatives had conducted many quick in-and-out operations for downed flyers in North Vietnam, but not for POWs already under detention. Nothing like the magnitude of the planned Son Tay raid had ever been contemplated during the Vietnam conflict.

The November 1970 operation into North Vietnam was to rescue 60 American POWs at the Son Tay prison camp, 23 miles from Hanoi. To pull it off, Blackburn knew he needed experienced Special-Forces troops and ARRS helicopter pilots skilled in behind-the-lines operations. The ground force commander of the rescue operation, code-named Ivory Coast (a name chosen at random by a Pentagon computer), was none other than Bull Simons, whose operational philosophy remained 'The more improbable something is, the surer you can pull it off.'

Simons handpicked a 59-man assault force divided into three groups, choosing SOG veterans to command two; Simons himself would lead the third. The Son Tay raiders trained at the ARRS home base, Elgin AFB, Florida, practicing on a full-scale Son Tay mock-up of lumber and target cloth that could be rolled up during daylight hours to mask the true nature of the operation from the twice-daily overflights of Soviet COSMOS spy satellites. Air support for the raiders included A-1E 'Sandy' attack planes, several C-130 'Combat Talons,' and HH-3 and HH-53 'Jolly Green Giant' choppers. Four months after planning began, intelligence reports noted 'decreased activity' at Son Tay. As the raid's launch window approached, Son Tay planners received two confusing pieces of intelligence. Photos from SR-71 reconnaissance planes indicated that 'someone' had reoccupied Son Tay, but even as the raiders moved into final positions in November 1970, a reliable North Vietnamese source passed to a Western agent a cigarette pack containing a list of active POW camps in the North. Son Tay was not on the list.

Nonetheless, the raid was given the 'Go.' Simons' men executed a near-perfect night assault on Son Tay. The only real flaw in the raiders' operation was fortuitous: Simons' chopper touched down in the wrong compound, marked on the map as a secondary school. In fact, before Simons could re-embark for the right camp, his 22-man force took under fire a large number of well-armed non-Vietnamese, possibly Communist Chinese, killing between 100-200. This error, which Simons later jokingly referred to as 'a pre-emptive strike,' probably saved the main raiding party from attack by an unexpected ground force. In the right camp, after a fierce fire-fight, the raiders discovered that the area contained no POWs. Simons safely brought out all 56 of his commandos. Total casualties were a broken ankle and a flesh wound.

The Son Tay exploit showed that highly trained Special-Forces raiders could penetrate deep inside North Vietnam and return with relative impunity. The US Army sent a top clandestine intelligence officer, former SOG operative Sully Fontaine, to check his contacts to determine, first, enemy reaction to the raid, and second, whether there had been a security leak that resulted in the Son Tay 'dry hole' (there was none). Talking to French, Polish and Soviet intelligence contacts, Fontaine was amazed to discover that the Chinese were appalled that North Vietnamese defenses were so lax as to allow a small American unit almost inside their capital. Fontaine found the Soviets totally surprised by the raid and anxious to know where the American commandos would strike next. If the Americans

could hit Son Tay, the Soviet agent surmised, perhaps they could hit anything. The Russians apparently believed Son Tay to be the start of a new American 'get-tough' phase in Vietnam policy. They appeared especially concerned about a certain Soviet-built hydroelectric project at Lang Chi Dam, not far from Son Tay.

General Blackburn, who saw the Son Tay raid as a chance to prove just how vulnerable the North Vietnamese were to such raids, contended that US Special Forces could and should have conducted more raids on North Vietnamese hydroelectric dams, power stations and bridges – the very type of 'active sabotage' denied to American commandos after 1954.

Above: Operation Lam Son 719 put South Vietnamese forces in possession of thousands of enemy weapons that had been destined for use against their country. The communists also lost over 400 tanks and trucks during this allied incursion into Laos.
Below: A member of the 173rd Airborne Brigade takes cover during Operation Greeley in 1968.

Winning Hearts and Minds: 1960-75

Pacification in Vietnam went under many different labels: civic action, strategic hamlets, revolutionary development, and perhaps the most interesting catch phrase, 'winning hearts and minds' (WHAM). But most Americans had only a vague understanding of what pacification, or clearing a given region of all guerrillas and the insurgent infrastructure, really meant, and where it all fit in among the hovering choppers, artillery firebases and search-and-destroy tactics of the televised war.

Mention pacification in Vietnam and most Americans will conjure up several different images: an American Green Beret or a Marine inoculating peasant children and building schools (the 1960s equivalent of the 1940s GI passing out chocolate bars and nylon stockings), or sinister CIA agents stalking the night, terrorizing local villages as part of Phoenix. Another view emerged in the anti-war documentary *Hearts and Minds*, quoting a military advisor: 'When you grab them by the b - - - -, their hearts and minds will follow.'

WHAM: Theory & Practice

Actually, the popular images present only a distorted stereotype of what the village-level conflict known as 'the other war' was really about. The rural village provided communist guerrillas with concealment, food, clothing, intelligence and a vast pool of recruits. Many American combat commanders, military advisors, AID (Agency for International Development) workers, even religious groups, grappled unsuccessfully with the task of separating

guerrillas from the people. When all else failed, many frustrated combat commanders resorted to extreme measures, such as the flattening of Ben Suc.

The term 'revolutionary warfare' as first used by Mao Tse-tung in 1936 described his brand of rural-based insurgency. It combined traditional guerrilla warfare with the propagation of communist ideology; in short, revolutionary warfare was *political* warfare. It took a long time for Westerns to understand and devise counter-measures to this concept. British pacification efforts employed in Malaya during the 1950s are credited with the first real success against Mao's brand of political warfare. British methods focused on several techniques: anti-terrorist police actions, population- and food-control measures, special intelligence operations (including defector inducement), jungle tactics and patrols. These operations proved successful, if lengthy, due to the complete unity of command under a single British High Commissioner and a well-integrated police and intelligence apparatus co-ordinated by Sir Robert Thompson, the noted counterinsurgency expert. This contrasted sharply with the French pacification methods practiced about the same period, which were characterized by bureaucratic confusion and, some claim, incompetence.

The other often-cited example of a successful counterinsurgency is Edward Lansdale's anti-Huk campaign in the Philippines, which used intelligence, police and small-unit patrols much as the British had, plus Lansdale's political-action and psywar concepts. Many of these same techniques were later applied in Vietnam, but without enjoying widespread success, for many reasons. The first was

Previous pages: *A US Air Force U-10 drops thousands of surrender leaflets over enemy-held territory near Pleiku Air Base, Central Highlands. Over 100 such psywar missions were flown every month during 1967.*
Above: *A suspected Vietcong is interrogated.*
Opposite top: *Youthful members of the South Vietnamese Popular Forces.*
Opposite bottom: *A US Navy officer touring Marine positions in the Mekong Delta watches a Vietnamese family share a C-ration lunch with US troops.*

geography: South Vietnam was not physically isolated like the Philippines and Malaya. The long, permeable border with Laos afforded many entry points by which to evade even the strictest border surveillance and control. More than any other factor, this gave the guerrilla external support and sanctuary, a vital lifeline for any insurgency. Denial of the option to wage large-scale unconventional (even conventional) warfare against those sanctuaries (including North Vietnam, the Great Rear Base) by US policymakers rendered police/intelligence techniques ineffective. This, too, was a high-level political decision that placed an even greater burden on potentially effective counterinsurgency programs.

The second reason has to do with the internal South Vietnamese political scene. Well-meaning American programs (often hopefully labeled nation-building programs) were too often mired down in Saigon political squabbles, coups, countercoups and bureaucratic ineptitude. This was worsened by the desire to maintain the fiction that the South Vietnamese were forging ahead by themselves, aided only by American advice and matériel. Further, the Vietnamese proved very sensitive to American meddling in such internal politics as Vietnamese relations with the highland minorities. In all fairness, the United States asked the South Vietnamese to perform a monumental task for any poor third-world nation: to fight a communist revolutionary insurgency and build democracy simultaneously – under the scrutiny of Western media.

Most Catholics in South Vietnam, including Chinese refugees like Father Augustin Nguyen Lac Hoa (left), were militantly anti-communist. Father Hoa's parishioners, who called themselves Hai Yen (Sea Swallows), *were advised about village defense by MAAG after they fled from Red China.*

Still, many in the Kennedy Admistration felt that Diem abused American aid and did not reciprocate in kind with democratic reforms. As set down in the 1961 original Overseas Internal Defense Policy, President Kennedy approved a comprehensive counterinsurgency doctrine aimed at the nation-building process to protect the vulnerable third-world democracies from communist 'wars of national liberation.' But military assistance was only part of US counterinsurgency aid. The principal components of the Kennedy program included civic action, public safety assistance (training and equipping of civil police), mobile development units (efforts to improve the standard of living in rural third-world countries) and emergency agricultural and economic assistance in areas considered ripe for subversion by communist guerrilla groups. To implement this counterinsurgency program, Kennedy established a special National Security Council

(NSC) working group, the Special Group (Counterinsurgency).

From the start, Vietnam occupied a major role in Special Group (CI) deliberations. In an attempt to steer clear of politics, American pacification policies emphasized techniques, methods and tactics, while avoiding politics altogether. Such US civic action projects as building schools, restoring public facilities and providing simple security were very good. But their apolitical nature failed to counter the VC political action precept – the ideological and psychological indoctrination associated with an attractive social revolution. The VC peddled nationalism, land reform and social revolution; to ensure co-operation, they also utilized selective terror. The Americans and the South Vietnamese did not have a truly effective national program for political action, based on the need for social revolution or a vision of the future, to counter the Vietcong's until after Tet.

General Lansdale understood that American counterinsurgency programs in South Vietnam lacked the requisite thrust to thwart communist political action. In a 1964 *Foreign Affairs* article entitled 'Vietnam: Do We Understand Revolution?,' Lansdale compared Vietnam to the Philippines and Malaya, noting that for counterinsurgency to succeed 'There must be a heartfelt cause to which the legitimate government is pledged, a cause which makes a stronger appeal to the people than the communist cause.' What was required to win the allegiance of the peasantry and counter Vietcong pie-in-the-sky promises was a definitive land-reform program, economic improvement and, most important, security. There was a major catch, however: programs designed to win over the population needed the support of the populace to defeat Vietcong terrorism; however, the average Vietnamese was understandably reluctant to swear allegiance to

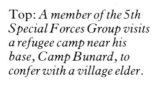

Top: *A member of the 5th Special Forces Group visits a refugee camp near his base, Camp Bunard, to confer with a village elder.*

Above: *A member of MACV gets acquainted with local children at Dang Tre.*

the Saigon Government until he felt more secure. The Vietcong made very sure that the peasantry did not feel secure enough to commit itself to full co-operation with Saigon.

Separating the guerrillas from the people was a good idea that had proven tactical applications. Unfortunately, early Vietnamese programs tended to be conceptually flawed and poorly executed. For many years, during the French colonial period, the Foreign Legion had practiced what were called 'oil-spot' pacification techniques. Beginning from a secure area and expanding outward, the Legion-naires would expel insurgent infestations and bring in security (sometimes brutally). An effective police informant network normally assisted them. Another French approach was that of Colonel LeRoy – essentially a tough guy with a knack for organization and a private army. The only problem with his approach was that it bred a 'city-boss' mentality and left plenty of room for abuse by power-hungry tyrants. In pacification, there was a fine line between effectiveness and trampling on basic human rights.

Diem tried a different approach to counter the communists: population resettlement in preselected areas where the government could more easily offer security. Diem's first major program along these lines, called Agrovilles, envisioned rural centers of economic development, political security and military communication – in short, an enlightened 'oil-spot' approach. Agrovilles were rural settlements of 400 families (2-3000 people), offering schools, hospitals, markets, even electricity. The program was a failure: only 23 Agrovilles were constructed before the program was abandoned due to mass peasant opposition.

Another of Diem's pacification projects, similar to Agrovilles, were 'Strategic Hamlets,' which also relied on population resettlement (sometimes by force). Again the peasants hated the program, resented forcible removal form their ancestral lands for 'their own good.' Strategic hamlets, launched with great fanfare by Diem's brother Nhu, also became a casualty of the American concept of 'measurable progress,' or progress by statistical indicators. Strategic hamlets were completed on paper, but were often little more than villages surrounded by barbed wire. Many were selectively targeted by the Vietcong – ironically, to reinforce the VC message that the Saigon Government was incapable of protecting the peasants. It wasn't long before the peasant had sworn alliegiance to Ho Chi Minh and was paying VC taxes.

Many pacification projects were wrecked from within by Vietcong 'moles' – part of a secret selected cadre that penetrated the South Vietnamese national army in 1954 at Hanoi's direction. Its long-term mission was to penetrate the highest ranks of the Saigon Government to ruin its relations with the peasantry. This included shielding local Vietcong cadres and sabotaging pacification projects.

One of the most flamboyant of these communist moles was Lt Colonel Pham Ngoc Thao, long considered one of the most dynamic and brilliant South Vietnamese military leaders. Thao was born into a wealthy Catholic family, but fought for the Viet-minh against the French. In 1955 Thao 'rallied' to Ngo Dinh Diem's anti-communist cause, and worked hard to flatter Diem and convince him of his trustworthiness.

These efforts were rewarded when Diem installed Colonel Thao as a province chief in Ben Tre, where he enthusiastically promoted Agrovilles, and later strategic hamlets, in this traditional communist stronghold. Thao's province soon became a showcase pacification project, the standard to which all others were compared. Western media wrote complimentary articles on Thao's handiwork, which looked so good only because he had a secret understanding with the local Vietcong leaders to keep hands off his model projects.

Thao reciprocated by shielding the Vietcong military units in Ben Tre, allowing them to grow unmolested. While Thao's province was being held up to the world as a model, the VC (helped by the unpopularity of the forced relocations) destroyed Agrovilles and strategic hamlets in other provinces. In 1965 Thao died under mysterious circumstances, reportedly after being captured and tortured by Nguyen Van Thieu as a suspected CIA agent. Thao met his fate after fleeing from several of the 're-volving-door' governments of the post-Diem period. However, his own ego – perhaps enlarged by

A fortified village at Cu Chi bristles with barbed wire and deadly bamboo stakes embedded in a deep moat.

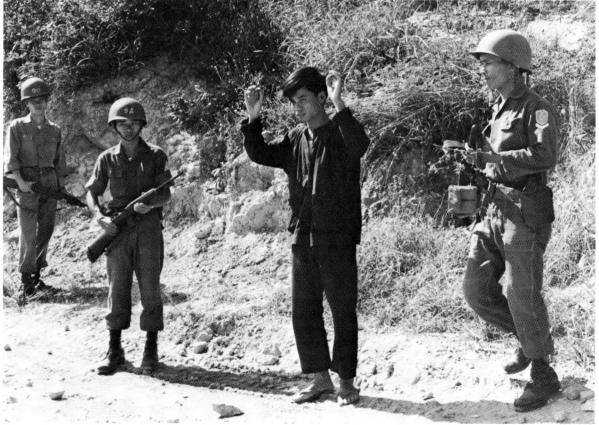

Above: *A Civil Defense fortification along Highway 1 in 1962.*
Left: *A young Vietcong surrenders to a Vietnamese Army patrol near Nha Trang, using an air-dropped surrender leaflet as a safe-conduct pass. In January 1966, over 1600 Vietcong defected in this way as a result of successful psywar operations.*

DEMAND THAT THE US GO_
VERNMENT STOP THE
WAR AND RESTORE PEA_
CE IN VIETNAM_CAMBODE

_JOIN WITH THE FOLKS AT
HOME FOR IMMEDIATE AND
COMPLETE TROOP WITHDRA
WAL FROM VIETNAM

W5c

A Vietcong propaganda sign found in Cambodia in June 1970 by members of the 11th Armored Cavalry.

The new US MACV commander in 1964, General Westmoreland, did however, give approval to an experimental 'oil-spot' program called Hop Tac (Co-operation) in September 1964 in III CTZ, around Saigon. The idea of Hop Tac was to expand governmental control in concentric circles from the Saigon suburbs outward to rural villages, creating enclaves of secured territory. The program enjoyed only modest success due to VC entrenchment outside the capital region, and political instability in Saigon, where military commanders placed key military units (often the best ones) on 'coup alerts.'

By mid-1965, the Vietcong reportedly controlled over 60 percent of South Vietnam's 12 million people, with some 40,000 VC cadres and 130,000 guerrillas. The 230,000-man ARVN, backed by 320,000 militia and police, had failed to guarantee even the security of American military advisors and installations, much less the Vietnamese population. With such a vast number of potential recruits, the Vietcong could keep the insurgency alive indefinitely.

The arrival of large US conventional combat forces overshadowed pacification; the emphasis was on sending American units charging after the elusive communist Main Forces. ARVN was relegated to the 'other war' in the villages, on theory that they were better equipped to do the job. By 1966 approximately 50 ARVN battalions – half of all ARVN combat units – were engaged in pacification operations (many in conjunction with RF/PF companies). But many Americans felt the ARVNs merely conducted 'search-and-evade' missions and were not eager to take on an enemy engaged in a far more sophisticated type of warfare.

Many of the most effective pacification projects in Vietnam were those undertaken by the American CIA, often as outgrowths of local CIA 'political actions.' The CIA philosophy in this sphere can be traced back to General Lansdale and his early psy-war techniques, shaped by international experience. Central to the idea of anti-communist political action was a counterorganization, seeded by grassroots involvement and CIA funds. Success, then, visited CIA projects not because Agency operatives were necessarily brighter, more creative, or more motivated than military advisors or AID personnel, but because the CIA was unburdened by either budgetary restraints or bureaucratic red tape.

The early CIDG program began as a CIA experiment. The first Village Defender project at Buon Enao was perhaps the best example of a successful pacification program. The concept was extremely simple: 'Give them something to fight for and something to fight with.' According to a 1965 CIA report on development of the CIDG program, 'Almost overnight we found we had inadvertently hit on a people-winning operation.... Recognizing its potential, we went ahead with it, developing concepts and doctrines, policies and procedures as the need for them arose, and changing them overnight when they did not fit a new development. We were not sure what the people had in mind...but they were going the way we wanted them to go, *i.e.*, against our common enemy.'

In planning the Village Defender program, CIA operatives studied all available communist material, including that by Vo Nguyen Giap: 'Our solution

the glare of international attention – may have figured in his downfall. Thao was a inveterate coup-maker, always plotting to overthrow the government in power. But there was little doubt that Thao's mission as a VC agent was to antagonize peasants and alienate them from the Saigon Government. In the intrigue-filled world of Saigon politics, Thao was just one of perhaps hundreds of secret communist agents or double agents covertly working against American counterinsurgency objectives.

In the wake of confusion after the overthrow of Diem in 1963, pacification programs faltered and died. The VC surged rapidly into the vacuum; Vietcong control of the countryside (aided by the infiltration of NVA regulars starting in 1964) spread dramatically. MACV advisers had rejected several Vietnamese pacification concepts put forward to revive the 'oil-spot' approach, because they seemed either too cautious or passive, surrendered the military initiative to the communists and took too long to implement. In 1964-5, MACV had little time to think about civic action and peasant hearts and minds: as Ambassador Maxwell D Taylor put it, 'The Indians were coming in the window.' The ARVN had been trained to seize the initiative and undertake offensive operations, and that was the MACV game plan.

was to use these same proven principles against the Vietcong and reinforce their application by better support, better organization and sincerity of purpose.' The CIA historian went on to note that the CIDG was 'essentially a very simple program. There were, of course, mistakes and failures. The outstanding mistake was to name it a paramilitary program. This brought in many official people who were interested primarily in the man with a gun and whom he could shoot, rather than the man.'

The CIA history indicates that when the CIDG program was turned over to the military under Operation SWITCHBACK, the original purpose – village defense and local involvement in resisting Vietcong influence – was distorted by the militaristic and offensive bend given the program by the Green Berets. Nevertheless, the CIA's CIDG concepts were not applied elsewhere as they could have been. The CIDG was not accepted by South Vietnamese because it dealt with native *Moi*, the highland 'savages,' or stepped on too many bureaucratic toes. Perhaps even communist moles like Colonel Thao, planted in Saigon, rejected it because it was so effective in countering the Vietcong.

In the populous Mekong Delta, the CIA sponsored several local pacification projects as part of its political-action programs of the early 1960s. Such ad hoc programs borrowed heavily from Lansdale's Philippine experience. In Kien Hoa Province (Colonel Le Roy's former bastion), CIA operatives formed 'Census-Grievance Teams,' which combed the Mekong hamlets to conduct a government

Above: *A CIDG member runs for cover, as NVA soldiers launch a mortar attack in 1969.*
Left: *An ARVN soldier destroys a propaganda sign posted in the jungle as he searches out Vietcong guerrillas.*

175

census and hear out peasant complaints while recruiting government agents and identifying local Vietcong. Another CIA political action in Kien Hoa involved 'Special Intelligence Teams,' disguised as ordinary farmers but armed with 9mm pistols, which performed similar functions. They acted as a private intelligence service, reporting directly to the province chief, Colonel Tran Ngoc Chau (who suspected the presence of agents among his staff). A talented officer, Chau himself was suspected of being a VC agent because his brother was a well-known colonel in the North Vietnamese secret service. Chau was later arrested by President Nguyen Van Thieu in 1967 for this reason, and other 'transgressions.'

More action-oriented political action groups in Kien Hoa were the 'Counter-Terror Teams' (or 'X-Teams'), which used local intelligence collected by the other pacification teams to take out local communist leaders. X-Teams specifically targeted the Vietcong Infrastructure (VCI) by employing favorite enemy tactics – kidnapping, ambush, assassination. Such tactics, which treated VC terrorists in kind, achieved local success and foreshadowed the Phoenix operations of the late 1960s.

Another example of trial-and-error success was the CIA seeding of the 'Cinnamon-and-Shrimp Irregulars,' a 500-man private paramilitary group formed in the early 1960s by a wealthy Saigon businessman at President Diem's behest. The irregulars' mission was to keep the Saigon-to-Vung-Tau highway open to the commercial fish and spice trade. Most of the irregular commanders were northern Catholics with previous combat experience and knowledge of communist guerrilla tactics from

fighting the Vietminh. This small force received CIA assistance after the VC tried to end their modest enterprise for preserving capitalism. The Agency armed the black-pajama irregulars with Thompson M3 submachine 'Grease guns,' recoilless rifles and mortars. After some expansion, the cinnamon-and-shrimp irregulars widened their areas of operation to contest VC sanctuaries, and co-operated with the 5th ARVN Division by screening their operations. The 5th ARVN commander, then-Colonel Nguyen Van Thieu, was impressed with the combat capabilities of the small mobile units. Eventually, their training camp outside Vung Tau would become the hub of a 5000-man training complex for the national 'Revolutionary Development' Program. Although small and decentralized, these early pacification projects developed counterinsurgency techniques applied on a national scale a few years later.

Vietcong terrorism continued to be a serious problem, with over 8000 government officials and community leaders assassinated between 1964-7. The Vietcong were succeeding in driving home the message to the peasantry that Saigon could not protect them adequately. One unlikely group of Americans contributed to the short list of successful pacification experiments. In August 1965, US Marines began an imaginative program that married civic action with the area-security concepts of the old CIDG. Experimental Combined Action Platoons (CAPs) matched a 14-man US Marine rifle squad and a US Navy corpsman (all volunteers who passed a strict screening process) with a 38-man Popular Forces platoon. The CAP was responsible for the security of a specific village (normally a cluster of hamlets averaging about 3500 people).

Above: *The port of Vung Tau was a training center for the Revolutionary Development Program (1966).*
Opposite top: *Both men and women joined guerrilla forces of the North and South in the war for Vietnam.*
Opposite bottom: *A wounded US Navy officer is put on display with other prisoners of war for propaganda purposes.*

CAP Marines lived in the village to become familiar with (and trusted by) the local population. The experience allowed the Marines to get a feel for the local terrain and culture, perhaps a better understanding of village security problems first-hand, while the PFs got to work with the Marines and improve their familiarity with weapons and tactics. Villagers received long-needed security, civic-action benefits and a sense that government shared their concerns. VC guerrillas, realizing the long-term dangers CAP platoons posed to their infrastructure, tried to target them for elimination. However, PF combat skills, morale and willingness to fight improved under the experimental CAP program, proving that patience, experience, good equipment and small-unit leadership could make the difference between good soldiers and unreliable militia.

By 1966 there were 57 CAP platoons, climbing to 79 platoons by late 1967. While CAP villages averaged much higher security levels than non-CAP villages, MACV believed the innovative program drained precious manpower from the priority task of seeking and destroying enemy Main-Force units. Consequently, the CAP program remained small and was not expanded outside the US Marine Corps area of operations in I CTZ.

The problem with innovative pacification programs in Vietnam, as the CIA operatives discovered with the CIDG formula, was that they were soon drained of all content smacking of political action or – as the author of the CIDG history noted – 'smothered under an avalanche of organizations, rules, regulations, formalized concepts and conventional thinking.' The South Vietnamese Government contributed little to solving the problem.

Going To The Source: CORDS and Phoenix

Counterinsurgency was almost abandoned in 1965, when the US buildup of conventional forces began. But population security was still the underlying problem in dealing with well-dug-in insurgent infrastructures, particularly the communist 'Self-Defense Militia' – those clandestine part-time guerrillas who remained intact even if ARVN or US units made a sweep through a given village. Harsh 'meat-axe' approaches to removing the VC infrastructure that characterized operations like Ben Suc ('We had to destroy the town to save it') was more WHAM than 'winning hearts and minds.' More moderate methods were needed.

A major American pacification study made in 1966, called the PROVN Study, concluded that the objective of the war was to win the allegiance of the South Vietnamese people, and pointed out that their security was being neglected. Up to that point, the list of failed programs – Reconstruction, Agrovilles, Strategic Hamlets, New Life Hamlets, Hop Tac, Chien Thang (Victory), Rural Construction, Rural Reconstruction – all had that same goal. But with major backing from Lyndon Johnson's White House, the first national pacification effort in South Vietnam began in May 1967. The Civil Operations and Revolutionary Development Support (CORDS) Program signaled a new emphasis on pacification. CORDS oversaw several paramilitary programs designed to attack the Vietcong infrastructure. The CIA's old idea of a political grass-roots organization actively supported by Saigon was realized in the Revolutionary Development (RD) concept that featured both political content and ideas to improve population security. Motivated RD cadre teams would go into a village to show how government cared about the peasant's personal security and improving his lifestyle. The objective was to give the average peasant a reason to fight for and support the government.

At the CIA's old 'Cinnamon-and-Shrimp' training camp at Vung Tau, an RD Center was established to train 59-man cadre teams to move about the countryside. Vietnamese Information Service (VIS) and *Son Truong* cadres (armed propaganda teams) performed similar RD functions. These were viewed at first with suspicion, and many were targeted for assassination or kidnapping by local Vietcong terror squads. But the RDs did begin the hard, slow task of winning over the population.

The first director of CORDS, Robert Komer, was dispatched directly from the White House staff, giving the ambassadorial-level position a Presidential stamp of approval. Komer was a bureaucratic cage-rattler who disliked red tape. But he did get results. He soon was given the nickname 'Blowtorch Bob' for shaking up the US Embassy in Saigon. The Vietcong gave him a different nickname, 'the sly old fox,' which showed grudging respect for CORDS. On the Vietnamese end of CORDS was Colonel Nguyen Be, a former Vietminh who had rallied in 1954, and who had been picked out by CIA talent scouts as one who understood the problems of pacification. Colonel Be helped organize the RD Program and ran the Vung Tau Center, which

turned out RD cadres in black pajamas.

Under 'Blowtorch Bob' Komer, CORDS launched an effort to improve the training and equipment of the RF/PF militia (the 'Ruff-Puffs'), revamp and restrengthen the National Police (a constabular force), accelerate the *Chieu Hoi* (Open Arms) defector program and mount a new attack of the VCI. After the communists' 1968 Tet Offensive decimated and exposed the Vietcong insurgent infrastructure, Saigon moved quickly with an Accelerated Pacification Campaign to fill the vacuum. Improved Regional and Popular Forces embarked on ambitious 'clear and hold' operations which took their toll on the VCI. The combination of the disastrous Tet Offensive and CORDS uprooted a great deal of the communists' infrastructure, making possible major gains in security in the countryside.

Another indicator of the population's greater faith in the government (and the government's in them) was the mobilization and arming of a 1.5-million-strong People's Self-Defense Force (PSDF) in 1969. The PSDF grew to about four million in 1971, with over 500,000 arms issued. Creation of the PSDF was made possible by the upgrading of the Ruff-Puff militia. Combined RF/PF operations with US troops on a regular basis led to a much greater appreciation of these forces by the Americans. By

Above: *Members of the US Army hand out parcels of food and clothing to needy South Vietnamese villagers.*
Opposite: *Members of Team A-29, Special Forces, pour diesel oil over captured small-arms ammunition before burning it.*
Right: *Armed Propaganda Teams march in formation.*

TRUNG·TÂM CHIÊU·HÔI BÌNH·TUY

Right: *A group of prisoners under guard.*

1971 the RF/PF paramilitary forces constituted 51 percent of all South Vietnamese military strength, with about 95 percent possessing the modern M-16 automatic rifle.

An apparent sign of the growing effectiveness of the territorial RF/PF forces was the effort the Vietcong put into infiltrating secret cadres into the territorial forces (as they had with ARVN) via the *Chieu Hoi* 'rallier' program in 1970. This attempt to subvert both the territorials and discredit the successful *Chieu Hoi* programs was recognized early in 1971, when several RF/PF outposts were overrun amid signs of collusion between attackers and defenders.

A major effort was made in 1967 to upgrade the effectiveness of the national police by creating a system of law enforcement in rural areas. The rural constabulary grew from 53,000 in 1965 to over 120,000 in 1972, most belonging to the paramilitary National Police Field Force and the Provincial Reconnaissance Units (PRUs) engaged heavily in anti-VCI operations. These groups led a much-publicized campaign known as the *Phuong Hoang* (Phoenix) Project, a CIA-directed effort to improve intelligence collection on the VCI begun in 1967. The stated objective of the Phoenix campaign was the 'neutralization' of the VCI – an ambiguous term open to varying interpretations even today. To the

Below: *Volunteers from a Vietnamese village assemble for a patrol against the Vietcong.*

Phoenix program, 'neutralize' meant those VC cadres captured, rallied (under *Chieu Hoi*) or killed.

However, in its relatively short bureaucratic existence (1968-71), Phoenix acquired an international reputation as a 'CIA assassination campaign,' perhaps because of the central role in its formation of Komer's deputy at CORDS (and later successor), William Colby, a career CIA official. Colby had a long history as a Cold War clandestine operative. He twice parachuted behind German lines for the OSS during World War II, later joined the CIA, and ran the Agency's Operation HAY-LIFT, the covert agent drops into North Vietnam in the early 1960s. Colby would later go on to become CIA director during the Agency's turbulent Watergate period. As CORDS chief, Colby represented not merely the CIA, but a multi-agency advisory group. Nevertheless, Phoenix would always have 'the CIA assassination program' link in the public's mind. Colby claims that the number of VC killed never exceeded 40 percent of the total number 'neutralized.' Some 17,000 cadre were captured under Phoenix; another 12,000 accepted amnesty under *Chieu Hoi*. About 20,000 people actually died under Phoenix operations, most during the course of normal military and police actions. Some historians even indicate that many of that total were not on the Phoenix VCI list, but died in unrelated military operations. They were added to the Phoenix total as a result of the ghoulish obsession with 'body counts' that characterized the American attempt to quantify 'victory.' Most 'neutralized' cadre were low-ranking VC who were usually captured, interrogated, then released. Another problem was that for some informants pointing an accusing finger, Phoenix was a method of settling personal vendettas and old scores. But some high-ranking VC cadres clearly were targeted for assassination. Average Americans were shocked at (perhaps exaggerated) Phoenix assassination reports. Unfamiliar with the underlying political nature of the systematic Vietcong terror that characterized the war, they objected to having their government officially sponsor activities of dubious morality.

National Police and PRU units served as the major enforcement arm of Phoenix, although the PRUs gained the most notoriety. The CIA-financed PRUs were airborne-qualified irregulars trained and supervised by 50 US Special Forces at the PRU training center in My Tho. The PRUs excelled in unconventional tactics, often working closely with such American special-warfare units as the US Navy SEALs in Mekong Delta communist strongholds.

The SEALs 'went native' in their work with the

South Vietnamese troops display a communist anti-aircraft weapon captured in Laos during Operation Lam Son 719 (1971).

Above: *An allied US Navy SEAL team patrols an inland waterway in 1968.*
Opposite: *Members of a Mobile Strike Force ford a muddy stream south of Ban Me Thuot – 1969.*

PRUs, going barefoot in black pajamas with blackened faces. Much attention was placed on learning to walk, move and think like VC; the objective was to blend in with the environment, crawling in and out of the jungles and delta marshes as the VC did. Since anti-VCI work was so dangerous, and the possibility of capture great, SEALs supposedly carried with them a vial of morphine. In the event a SEAL was wounded or captured, he could inject himself and become incoherent for 24 hours – long enough for the parent team to change codes, signals and plans. Some SEAL 'green-faced frogmen' even took dexedrine ('speed') to increase their sensory perceptions in the jungle, turning themselves, according to one account, into 'a pair of eyeballs and ears.' The PRU reputation for aggressiveness and rowdiness fostered rumors that Provincial Reconnaissance Units were recruited from South Vietnamese jails. Their background aside, the PRUs were considered, man-for-man, the most effective anti-VCI unit in South Vietnam.

End of a Covert-War Era

'Vietnamization' and the increased emphasis on pacification after the 1968 Tet Offensive coincided with the drawdown of American combat forces. After Tet, the Vietcong insurgency that characterized the earlier phase of the war had changed. Academics may debate whether this resulted from the decimation of the VC in Tet and the follow-up pacification efforts, or from a deliberate communist decision, but subsequent major communist offensives in 1972 and 1975 were largely conventional affairs, with an increased use of big maneuver units,

heavy artillery and tanks by both the ARVN and the NVA.

Because of their familiarity with local communist supply bases in Cambodia and Laos, Projects Omega and Sigma did see action during the 1970 Cambodian and 1971 Laotian incursions. These were marginal efforts – really too little, too late – to clear out COSVN and major communist supply depots threatening South Vietnam. A few former special-recon and SOG operatives returned during th NVA's 1972 Easter Invasion to penetrate enemy territory again, in order to call in American airstrikes – including massive B-52 bombings to support ARVN ground units.

But it was a last hurrah. Five months after the Son Tay POW raid into North Vietnam, US Special Forces ended their role in the CIDG program; those CIDG units became either ARVN Rangers or LLDB regulars, as originally planned back in 1964. And on 1 March 1971, the 5th Special Forces Group (Airborne) struck its colors and redeployed back to Fort Bragg. The Special Forces left Vietnam earlier than many American regulars, partly because Westmoreland's successor, the gruff tanker General Creighton 'Abe' Abrams, was not a big fan of the Green Berets, partly because the Special Forces had sunk so low in the public esteem. Perhaps because the Green Berets had once symbolized America's commitment to Southeast Asia, their reputation sank comparatively lower than that of the average US soldier. 'Counterinsurgency' was no longer in vogue, and the Special Forces faced a long, agonizing period out in the cold.

A large American military presence in Southeast Asia guaranteed that Air America (and its CIA spon-

sors) could operate in relatively obscurity. With little fanfare during the war, the CIA proprietary airline had covertly fought on the front lines of America's unconventional war. In its glory days, Air America fed numerous clandestine guerrilla armies, acting as both an aerial guerrilla force and the CIA's commuter airline of the Far East. As the war expanded, AA pilots continued to fly the most hazardous black projects in 'sanitized' aircraft from numerous secret bases in Thailand, Laos and Vietnam – many for the thrill of it and an envelope stuffed with cash. Other AA pilots flew in virtually every type of aircraft imaginable, transporting everything from combat troops to baby chicks, dropping everything from food to starving refugees to Nung trailwatchers onto the Ho Chi Minh Trail. With its bizarre form of pragmatism, AA contracted with the Drug Enforcement Agency to track international drug traffic and with the Meo to haul their annual opium crop.

As the US pulled out of Vietnam, Air America picked up much of the slack, and strained to maintain the status quo. It was not easy. When the United States made known its diplomatic intentions to wind down its military involvement, strong and confident NVA and Pathet Lao forces took the offensive in the early 1970s, driving out the Meo from their ancestral homelands. As the once-strong Meo retreated, Air America found itself hauling and feeding tens of thousands of refugees in an attempt to live up to its long-ago promise not to abandon the Meo as the French had. Domestically, the CIA fell under intense Congressional scrutiny of its worldwide clandestine paramilitary activities. Pressure grew to divest itself of Air America and its built-in capability to support CIA 'political action.'

South Vietnam collapsed rapidly in 1975, following a Congressional cut-off of military aid to the South Vietnamese Army and a major NVA conventional military campaign – the 'Great Spring Victory.' However, it was not a barefoot guerrilla who led the final victory in a 'people's war,' but rather a Russian-made tank that crashed through the gates of the presidential palace in Saigon in April 1975. The last days of South Vietnam – which saw Air America involved, as in 1954, in a mass evacuation – signified the end of a major clandestine phase of the Cold War that had begun in 1945.

Communist crewmen operate a North Vietnamese Army anti-tank rocket launcher in the ongoing war for Indochina (1982).

Above: *American flyers soon learned to be wary of North Vietnamese marksmanship with the 37mm anti-aircraft gun. The French had learned the same lesson in the 1950s.*
Left: *A victorious communist soldier carries the Khmer Rouge flag through the streets of Phnom Penh on 17 April 1975, when the Cambodian Army surrendered to the communists.*
Following pages: *Crewmen of the USS* Blue Ridge *push a Vietnamese helicopter into the sea to make room on the landing deck for additional aircraft carrying refugees from Saigon and environs in April 1975.*

Epilogue

In the late twentieth century, the name 'Vietnam' has come to symbolize a 'dirty' unconventional war between a relatively small number of irregulars and a vastly superior conventional power. Inevitably, this tag implies that the superior military force – with its artillery, tanks and road mobility – becomes bogged down in an unwinnable war, while the tenacious guerrillas, overcoming all odds, prevail.

Today such unconventional war scenarios apply not only to Western 'imperialists,' but to communist powers as well. Continuing guerrilla insurgencies against communist regimes in Angola, Ethiopia, Afghanistan, Nicaragua and Cambodia demonstrate that Marxist-Leninists do not hold a monopoly on guerrilla warfare. Even the Soviet Union, the original sponsor of wars of national liberation, found its own Vietnam during the 1980s in the rugged mountains of Afghanistan, where almost 100,000 Russian troops desperately tried to prop up a wobbly communist regime with fighter-bombers, helicopter gunships and tanks. Eerily reminiscent of America's Vietnam, Soviet and puppet Afghan troops control the cities and towns, venturing out only in heavily protected convoys and helicopter-gunship escorts, while lightly armed Mujahideen guerrillas control the countryside and operate at will after dark.

In Africa, Moscow's favorite proxy troops, Fidel Castro's Cuban 'Africa Corps,' struggle against non-communist Angolan guerrillas of Joseph Savimbi's UNITA, who hold their own against the Cubans and the Marxist government troops. Savimbi's anti-communist Angolan forces hold major portions of the countryside, despite withdrawal of American aid in 1975.

The greatest irony, however, is the transformation of Ho's Vietnam into an 'imperialist aggressor' in its own right. In 1975 Hanoi's juggernaut not only conquered the South, but swallowed up 'neutral' Laos. It invaded neighboring Communist Cambodia (Kampuchea) in 1978, expelling the blood-thirsty Khmer Rouge regime of Pol Pot. Today, Vietnamese settlers flood Cambodia like Asian carpetbaggers, to lay claim to ancient Khmer territory.

But Cambodia has proven to be Vietnam's Vietnam. Several Cambodian guerrilla fronts (two non-communist groups, plus the Khmer Rouge) battle the 160,000-man Vietnamese occupation force, employing well-worn jungle tactics used by the old Vietminh and Vietcong. For their part, Hanoi's generals have assumed the role of the US Army. Vietnamese troops routinely employ armor (Soviet T-54 tanks), massed artillery barrages and motorized infantry. Like the old US MACV, Vietnamese operations are curtailed by terrain and monsoon weather. Unlike MACV, Vietnamese troops are not hesitant to cross into Thailand in hot pursuit of Cambodian insurgents, and frequently clash with crack Thai Rangers on the border. In seven years, however, Hanoi's powerful army has not crushed the insurgency. In addition, Hanoi's brand of imperialism has resulted in a falling out with Communist China, its recent benefactor (but ancient enemy). Since 1979, Vietnamese and Chinese forces have engaged in repeated border clashes and artillery duels at 'Friendship Pass' in Langson Province, where Vietminh guerrillas once accepted captured US arms from Mao.

The Great Spring Victory of 1975 brought anything but peace to Southeast Asia. Besides occupying Cambodia, Hanoi still wages war against the Meo (Muong) people with the estimated 80,000 Vietnamese troops in Laos. The Meo, abandoned twice in 20 years by both France and America, endure continued communist harassment and terrorism, including reported attacks with chemical weapons ('yellow rain') supplied by the Soviet Union. (It is perhaps no coincidence that anti-communist Afghan guerrillas also claim that the deadly yellow rain has visited their villages.)

Armed resistance inside Vietnam itself has not ended. Reports in the West from refugees and occasional press items indicate that extensive low-level resistance, in the form of small-unit attacks and ambushes, continue. The most active resistance appears to come from the highlands in the tri-border region of the old Ho Chi Minh Trail, where *Montagnards* (including old CIDG strikers) have a long history of resisting ethnic Vietnamese incursions. Experts believe that even the North Vietnamese Army, despite its known brutality, has had little success in subjugating the tough mountain people.

Some former South Vietnamese went underground after 1975, or have since returned home to take up arms against the communists. Other armed opposition reportedly includes such religious minorities as the Hoa Hao and the Cao Dai, and even former Vietcong disillusioned by the northern regime. In 1982, CBS News reported on one small resistance band, led by a former South Vietnamese admiral named (evocatively enough) Hong Co Minh, which had adopted old Vietcong tactics, right down to the pungi stakes, booby traps and political indoctrination sessions.

Various Vietnamese resistance groups claim between 20-22,000 armed insurgents scattered about central and southern Vietnam, (generally within the arc of the old Ho Chi Minh Trail). These guerrilla groups, financed by Vietnamese refugee communities worldwide, lack efficient co-ordination and a big-power sponsor to make them truly effective. Nevertheless, ten years after the fall of Saigon, guerrilla war continues to play a major role in Southeast Asian politics.

The legacy of those Vietnam 'secret warriors' who returned to the United States is renewed interest in the potential of irregular warfare in preparing for low-level conflicts and contingencies around the world. In the 1980s, America has seemingly awakened to the twin threats of communist insurgency in Central America and international terrorism, symbolized by the disasters in Nicaragua, Iran and Lebanon. 'The United States as a superpower has become increasingly incapable and impotent at the low end of the spectrum,' one high-ranking military officer remarked in 1984, citing the need to adapt to low-level and unconventional military con-

The helicopter zone at the US Embassy, Saigon, during last-minute evacuation of authorized personnel and civilians from the doomed South Vietnamese capital (29 April 1975). Air America played a major role in the mass evacuation, closing the circle it had opened up in 1954.

tingencies. Special-operations forces have been reborn in such units as Delta Force, the US Army's elite counterterrorist unit. Revitalized Special Forces and SEALs are now trained as essential components in a US unconventional warfare posture, not as mere 'hot dogs' or prima donnas. The US Army has formed the 1st Special Operations Command; the Air Force followed suit in 1983, with formation of the 23rd Air Force. In 1984 the JCS created the Joint Special Operations Agency to co-ordinate all special-forces activities and manage a top-secret, all-service, rapid-deployment commando unit, an organization reminiscent of SOG. Reportedly, two old Polaris nuclear-missile submarines have been adapted for use by these forces.

In late 1984, NBC News created a minor sensation when it reported that highly classified, specially trained Green Beret units in Germany were deployed with lightweight 'nuclear backpacks' (150-pound atomic demolition mines) designed to cripple a

Warsaw Pact breakthrough in Western Europe by operating behind enemy lines. The Reagan Administration has given strong support to rebuilding unconventional special-operations capabilities and voiced general support for the concept of US covert aid to anti-communist insurgencies. The Central Intelligence Agency has supported clandestine insurgents in Nicaragua and Afghanistan (to mention the most visible operations). Re-emphasis on US covert aid to non-communist 'freedom fighters' around the globe reflects an attitude that the West too can play 'the guerrilla game' (despite a lack of general support on the public's part). According to the veterans, however, we must also begin to think in terms of unconventional strategies in which to apply these capabilities, remembering that in Vietnam irregular units served as tactical appendages to a conventional military approach.

In the post-Vietnam period, Americans have had difficulty viewing such situations in strategic terms, seeing them instead strictly in terms of the moral consequences of 'another Vietnam.' As the world's most powerful democracy, the United States has the responsibility of formulating national security policies with the latter in mind, but we cannot neglect to consider the former as well. To do so is to ignore the painful lesson of unconventional war learned in Indochina and to invite another Vietnam we hope to avoid.

Index

Numbers in italics indicate illustrations

Photo Credits

Photographs for this book were supplied by the US Defense Department, with the following exceptions:
Associated Press/Wide World Photos: 4-5, 11 (bottom), 26-7, 38, 41 (right), 45 (below), 49, 50 (both), 51 (inset), 52-3 (all), 68 (left).
Bison Picture Library: 8 (bottom), 14, 16-17 (bottom), 54 (inset), 58 (below), 76.
FPG International: 6-7, 20, 22 (bottom), 30 (bottom), 33, 37 (right), 44, 46-7, 169 (top).
Robert Hunt Library: 18 (below), 20-21, 45 (above), 55 (inset), 58 (top), 128, 132, 168.
Lockheed-California Company: 108.
National Archives: 16 (top).
Orbis House: 9, 11, 13, 14-15, 16-17 (top), 18 (above), 22-3, 24 (left), 25 (bottom), 28, 29, 30-31, 34-5, 36-7, 40-41, 42, 43, 46 (top), 54-5.

Acknowledgments

The publishers would like to thank the following people who have helped in the preparation of this book: Michael Rose, who designed it; Robin L Sommer, who edited it; Mary R Raho, who did the photo research; Florence Norton, who prepared the index.